TO CLARE AND MILO

LONDON
IN FRAGMENTS
A MUDLARK'S TREASURES
TED SANDLING

FOREWORD BY IAIN SINCLAIR

F

FRANCES
LINCOLN

Frances Lincoln Limited
74–77 White Lion Street
London N1 9PF
www.franceslincoln.com

Quarto is the authority on a wide range of topics.

Quarto educates, entertains and enriches the lives of
our readers – enthusiasts and lovers of hands-on living.

www.QuartoKnows.com

The Thames foreshore can be a hazardous area and
special care should be taken while mudlarking and
exploring. Do check the times of the tides before
venturing out. Anyone going on the foreshore does
so entirely at their own risk; neither the author nor
the publisher can accept responsibility for any harm,
damage, loss or prosecution that may be claimed as
a consequence – directly or indirectly – of the use or
misuse of the advice given in this book.

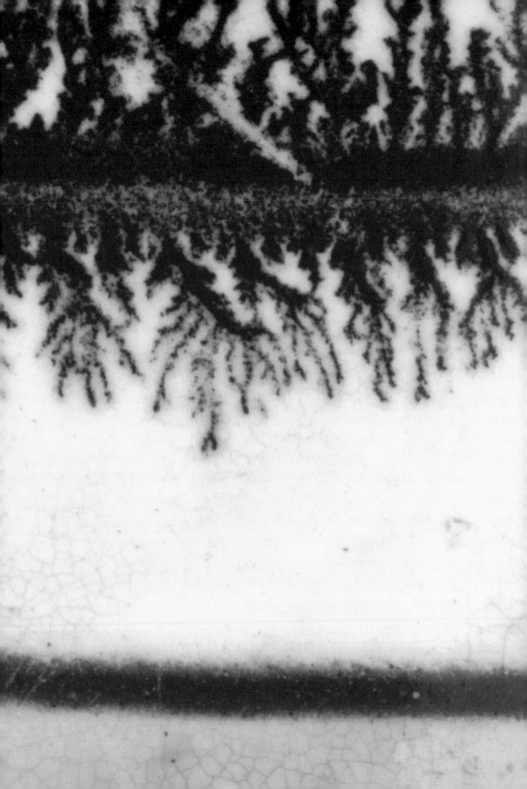

FOREWORD

Fired by Ted Sandling's adroitly curated account of mudlarking in crunching interstitial zones along the sole-sucking foreshore of the Thames, I came at low tide, in my heaviest boots, with a pocket of folded plastic bags, to the river steps below Tate Modern. This, as Sandling affirms, is a good place to start. Draw breath and acclimatise with a framed backdrop of heritage London. The grey whale-hump of Wren's cathedral, hedged in by never satisfied development, is emphasised today by the irregular migrainous thump of pile drivers attacking the mud. That elegant intervention, the Millennium Footbridge, is a teasing, hyper-budget reference to one of those wobbly vine cradles across the upper reaches of the Amazon. It is both an echoing catwalk of selfies and a way of avoiding the pluck and slap of the exposed beach. We have forgotten the risks that any crossing once involved. Tricky landing sites where wherries deposited Londoners with business among the brothels and theatres on the south side of the river.

Much of the approved Thames path, forever negotiating between private and public, opts for the virtual over the actual, thereby spurning the essence of what London has always been about: its river highway. That restless, sediment-heavy movement. The sound and smell of dying centuries. The pre-human gravity. To begin to understand the complexity of migration and settlement, patterns of trade, fashions in architecture, we have to learn to read the hard evidence, as it has been deposited on the foreshore. The impulse is forensic: bones, smoothed corners of brick, masonry nails, coins, relics hidden among gravel and coal bruises to tempt future detectorists and amateur historians. From these fugitive traces past lives can be assembled like novels missing vital chapters. In the golden hour, when the liquid carpet rolls back, we are free to comb and trawl without challenge, to carry home choice shards from which we can *almost* taste the biographies of those who were here before us. Sandling's book is the ideal companion for a day's speculative mudlarking. He offers practical information and a catalogue of seductive illustrations to complement scholarship and to promote the fetish for riparian scavenging as an honourable and long-standing tradition of place.

The practice of strolling and stooping, turning over likely stones with boots poulticed in noxious slop, is one of the surviving liberties of the city. At first, conscious of being watched by tourists and loungers, mudlarks wait for the familiar shout of the orange-gillet security guard. 'Excuse me, sir . . .'. If I were challenged among the generic fountains, outside City Hall, for having the impertinence to record my impressions by way of a small digital device, why should I be allowed to explore the exposed rubble and rotten pilings of the Thames foreshore? But on this special morning, in the afterglow of *London in Fragments*, anything seems possible. I remember the charge, twenty years ago, when the poet Brian Catling wobbled down wet steps alongside London Bridge to set up a brazier, on which he melted, in a huge ladle, all the lead type of his handset book, *The Stumbling Block*. A molten silver stream was poured into the river. It formed itself at once into a solid ball, hissing against the affronted wavelets, before disappearing from our astonished gaze.

Sadly, no alchemised lump of poetry was discoverable in the mud below Tate Modern. Sandling's much sharper eye identified a type block at Vauxhall with enough text remaining to stand as 'the most perfect description of a mudlark's dreams'. *GOLD . . . Handsome . . . graved, and . . . Pearls and fine . . . lustrous Gems.* The first lesson of the river is that we find what we need to find. Gnomic phrases confirm unresolved quests. Hints gleaned from *London in Fragments* led me to pick up objects I might otherwise have ignored. There were numerous stems of broken clay pipes, but nothing as striking as the horse's hoof pipe bowl Sandling bagged on an early outing. The disposable relics of Victorian smokers, like buried whispers from the novels of Charles Dickens, hold traces of the DNA of long-dead London working men who took time to contemplate the flux of the river. Beneath the notice of professional archaeologists, the cheap clay pipes invoke the thin wands laid across the chest of the young man excavated in 1823 by William Buckland from Paviland Cave in the Gower Peninsula, the oldest ritual burial in these islands.

I picked up the neck of a green-glass bottle. The jagged lip I knew was broken by design. Here was a container for ink, originally plugged by paper not cork, and snapped from a blowpipe. Ink for an unwritten book in the secret library of the city. There is something so attractive about parts of words on china, ceramic tiles, shards of industrial jugs and bottles. For years, I have been carrying home mutilated alphabets, sentences to be fitted together. It's like an endless game of post-architectural Scrabble. On the raised beach, below the promoted collections of Tate Modern, I make my own small exhibition, starting with letters on smoky glass: . . . *& CHIC* . . . *FFEE*. Trade goods: chicory, coffee. Miniature histories of colonial invasion and exploitation. And I gather up Chinese blue chips of tesserae, a temple floor still to be laid out. Morning-bright colours shine in dark slurry like beds of drowned forget-me-nots.

A few days later, still high on *London in Fragments*, I investigated the foreshore, upstream in Battersea, close to the church in which William Blake married Catherine Boucher. This second expedition confirmed the differences that are to be revealed in every stretch of the river. In Battersea, the slipway was decorated by single shoes and trainers hung in an unstable curtain from the mooring chains. There were no broken stems of clay pipes. There were no decorated blue tiles. And the only intact bottle that I captured was embossed with elephants, snake charmers, palm trees and a boat. 'Closer to Walt Disney than Vishnu,' said my companion, who did his best to crack the Hindi script. What we had picked up was a beer bottle, perhaps a votive gesture to the river, signalling a shift in the social demographic. The Battersea foreshore offers evidence of water ceremonies dedicated to Ganesh, from a festival held in September.

The joy of *London in Fragments* is that it takes us straight back to the founding myth of our city: why we are here, why we remain. The story has elements of Henry Mayhew's reportage, elements of a formidable cabinet of curiosities promoted by a generous collector. There are obvious parallels with the artist Mark Dion's memorable mudlarking project, *Tate Thames Dig*. Dion laid out a display without hierarchies or discriminations of plunder. Whatever was gathered up from the foreshore, beside Tate Britain at Millbank and Tate Modern at Bankside, could be categorised and labelled with the dignity of some august institution like the Pitt Rivers Museum in Oxford. Books dissolve in the bite of the river. But accidental junk, the jumble of vanished lives, is immortal. Ted Sandling lays out the map of his own obsessions and we become willing accomplices on an 'algorithmical' walk that will last until the waters cover our city.

Iain Sinclair

WHAT IS A MUDLARK?

A decade or so ago, I was showing some friends around London. They were visiting from Rome for the weekend. We'd gone shopping in Borough Market, to an exhibition at the still-new Tate Modern, then we walked back along the riverside to Waterloo. By Blackfriars Bridge, we stopped to look at the Thames and saw that the tide was out, exposing a wide gravel beach beneath us. I had been down there a few times before, not looking for much, never finding anything of interest, but enjoying being somewhere hidden in the centre of London. We decided to make it the final stop on our tour. Not knowing there was any other way, we climbed around a locked steel gate and down steps towards the river.

By Blackfriars the foreshore is solid to walk on. It's made of pebbles and architectural waste: broken bricks, cobbles, tiles and scaffold brackets. The water under the bridge recedes almost as far as the first pier. There, daylight is muted, sounds muffled. We stood beneath the span and looked up at girders and brackets and decorations. Then, with feet almost wet at the river's edge we stared across the water at the boats and the City of London. The Thames is omnipresent in our conception of London but it is nearly always viewed from a safe distance, from an embankment or a bridge. (Have you ever walked across the river and spontaneously breathed in, deeply? As if, somehow, passing over it has momentarily solved all your problems? Crossing a bridge I often catch myself sighing with an unexpected contentment.) But walking on its shore is like stepping into a different London. Breaking the boundary from river path to foreshore is unexpectedly transgressive; the beach seems a forbidden space.

Under the bridge, scuffing the gravel with my shoe, I touched an old clay tobacco pipe and picked it up. In places on the foreshore, pipe stems are everywhere. Even the first time I went down I picked up a dozen or more. I knew to look for the chalky white tubes, the broken stems of the eighteenth-century cigarette. Pipes were cheap, disposable, sometimes given away for free with a pinch of tobacco. They stand out against the round flint pebbles. But this one was more than a fragment; it had a bowl at the end, one of the first ones I'd ever found. And when I turned it over in my hands I saw that it was not just a bowl. It also had a well moulded shape to it; turned upside down it became a perfect horse's hoof, complete with a fetlock and a fine coat of hair (page 104).

Some might compare London unfavourably to Rome (occasionally they might be right: let's start with the weather). Rome is a city almost overwhelming in its antiquity. Yet although the ancient matter is everywhere, I dare you to try taking it home. Here, in the centre of London, below the drinkers of the Founders Arms, I was holding history: not of great political events, but of very small things, of an individual living around 1850 who had broken his pipe and chucked it in the river. There is a connection there, between him and me, a participation in the same story. Museums could show you a collection of pipes (I suspect it might be tedious), but these collections have been curated through generations, selected by experts and stifled behind glass. The same object, fresh from the beach, held for the first time in a hundred years, suddenly has a spark of life to it: it is fascinating because it is found, and because it is unmediated, and because of the vanishingly small number of individuals who have ever had it in their possession. I had suddenly and by chance become the most recent name on the list. Not to mention that it was *a clay pipe shaped like a horse's hoof*: I knew I wanted more of this.

But what was 'this'? It turned out that this was mudlarking. Today, mudlarking means searching the Thames foreshore for artefacts and antiquities. But it is an old name, maliciously descriptive. People hearing it for the first time often assume that it's mud-wrestling, that I'm doing it in budgie-smugglers in a paddling pool. It is not, but 150 years ago there would have been wrestling involved, though not for spectators' pleasure. Mudlarks fought each other, the authorities and the mud as they sought to recover scrap for a tiny, hard-earned profit. The River Thames today is not the river of then; it's not even the river of fifty years ago. It is a relic of past industry. Until its decline of the 1960s and 1970s, when containerisation made the London docks uneconomic and no longer deep enough for the vast ships plying global trade, the Thames was like Heathrow. It was a vital node at the centre of international trade and transport, with ships docking from everywhere, sailing to anywhere. The docks dug off the Thames were at the centre of advanced logistics; before they were built, all the massed tonnage of shipping landed at quays along the river. The queues to unload could last months; goods lined the wharves like barricades.

'Here, in the centre of London, below the drinkers of the Founders Arms, I was holding history: not of great political events, but of very small things, of an individual living around 1850 who had broken his pipe and chucked it in the river.'

Besides trade, the river was used for shipbuilding, to feed factories and for local transport. Until 1750, when Westminster Bridge was constructed, London Bridge was the only way to cross the river other than by boat. Wherries were the equivalent of taxis. It was almost always quicker to travel by water than by road, and the risk of robbery significantly diminished (except for a scalping from your oarsman). Contemporary pictures show the Thames seething, consumed by traffic. And all of this shipping and industry had one place for its waste: the river.

This is where we meet the original mudlarks: impoverished people barely surviving by salvaging scrap from the foreshore and selling it on to their dealer, called a dolly. I think the image typically conjured of a mudlark is an emaciated child forced into the grime, but mudlarks ranged from the very young to the very old. They were victims of the grotesque social structures of Victorian London, an overcrowded capital with strict segregation between the deserving ('hard working') and the undeserving poor. Yet few worked harder or in more miserable conditions than the mudlarks: all they were undeserving of was their circumstances. And yet, ignored by society, they eked out their living by scouring the foreshore when the tide was out, hoping to collect enough to make at most four pennies in a day. If we think the river is dirty today, it was a sewer then. Those mudlarks spent their days crouched in a cesspit.

Henry Mayhew, the most accessible and sympathetic of the anthropologists of the Victorian poor, gives us a detailed account of the mudlark's life in

'Few worked harder or in more miserable conditions than the mudlarks. Ignored by society, they eked out their living by scouring the foreshore when the tide was out, hoping to collect enough to make at most four pennies in a day.'

London Labour and the London Poor (1851). Not even clothed in rags, but 'half covered by tattered indescribable things that serve them for clothing; their bodies are grimed with the foul soil of the river, and their torn garments stiffened up like boards'. The world of the mudlarks that he describes lacks even a community. They are men and women that 'notice no one; they never speak, but . . . plash their way through the mire, their bodies bent down while they peer anxiously about'.

The original mudlarks were looking for items with an immediate resale value: coal, old iron, rope, copper rivets (see pages 160–1). Mayhew describes old women, bent double, taking a whole low tide to fill a battered tin kettle with pieces of coal or chips of wood. Interrogating a nine-year-old mudlark, he finds that the extent of his knowledge is that 'London was England, and England was in London', and yet he gives mudlarks such colour that his accounts become the barely disguised backbone of a book published a hundred years later, Theodore Bonnet's *The Mudlark*. There's not a lot of mudlarking; it's really a hymn to Disraeli, albeit needing an ingenious plot device to show the statesman at his very best. That device is the eponymous mudlark: a small boy called Wheeler, who hears that Queen Victoria is the mother of England, and makes his way up to Windsor Castle for some well deserved mothering. Unfortunately for him, Victoria has sequestered herself away after the death of Prince Albert and wants nothing more than that the public's demands of her go to the blazes.

Wheeler is discovered first behind the curtains as the Queen dines with Disraeli, and then by the Prime Minister in the throne room, on the throne, where the whisky-sodden gillie Mr Brown has taken him on a whisky-sodden tour of the palace. Disraeli uses the mudlark's story to unify the country, improve the lot of the poor, and bring Queen Victoria victoriously back to the nation's heart. I think it's a saccharine novel, but the story throws up the real social ills of Victoria's reign, and the author cares deeply. The book was turned into a film almost immediately, with Alec Guinness reprising his portrayal of a stereotyped Jew two years after playing Fagin. Much of the grinding poverty was lost, but the mudlark succeeds in liberating Victoria from her mourning.

Poor Jack, by the writer of sailors' romances, Captain Frederick Marryat, is another story with a young mudlark as its hero. Marryat was once hugely popular, his books on every schoolboy's shelves. They're the sort of novels I used to read in a day, never leaving the corner of the sofa. Having no idea how lucky I was or that I'd never be able to bring back that time again.

Type block
Nineteenth century (image flipped)

Reads:
GOLD
Handsome . . .
graved, and . . .
Pearls and fine . . .
lustrous Gems

I picked this off the shore at Vauxhall.
Somehow it saw into my heart: it is the most
perfect description of a mudlark's dreams.

Poor Jack was written when young mudlarks were active on the Thames –
in 1838, the year after Victoria was crowned. For Marryat, the poor have
made their beds and deserve everything they get but, untroubled by any
prim Victorian sensibilities, his ragged-trousered characters are filled with
the joys of dissipation, of brawling and drinking and adventure. Poor Jack
earns his halfpence not by scrounging in the mud, but by 'running into
the water, offering [his] ragged arm to people getting out of the wherries,
always saluting them with, "You haven't got never a halfpenny for poor Jack,
your honour?"' In this he resembles Mayhew's crossing-sweepers, clearing
the roads of manure for gentlefolk to cross (they too with the cry of 'give a
halfpenny to poor little Jack'). And it's a position to be fought for. Jack is
'often pushed away by those who were older and stronger than [him]self,
with a "go along with you! He's not poor Jack – I'm poor Jack, your honour."'

In *Poor Jack*, the pennies earned on the foreshore are sufficient to make
him independent and happy. The romance of the river translates into a
pilotship, and then wealth and comfort. For a rags-to-riches story, a mudlark
provides some most appealing rags to start with. While it is a better read
than Bonnet's *Mudlark*, I fancy that Marryat's Poor Jack was nigh on unique
among mudlarks in transcending his rags and discovering his riches.

And yet Marryat shows that there were more roles for the mudlark than
just scavenging for scrap. And seeing that there is something to the river
beyond coal and rivets takes us closer to the contemporary mudlark, because
an easy way to earn beer money, as Ivor Noël Hume delights in repeatedly
putting it in his 1956 book *Treasure in the Thames*, was to find antiquities and
to sell them to collectors and dealers.

Noël Hume was one of the pioneers of historical archaeology, a sort of
archaeological social history, and a great interpreter of London's history.
It's sixty years since Noël Hume wrote that book, and it remains possibly
the only one devoted to the archaeology of the river, which is astonishing,
because the River Thames has given us some of the most important artefacts
of Roman and Pre-Roman Britain, such as that masterpiece of Iron Age
metalwork, the Battersea Shield, now in the British Museum, found during
the mid-nineteenth century construction of Chelsea Bridge.

That was in the golden age of mudlarking, and that age has passed. In
the nineteenth century, the Thames underwent multiple transformations.
Bridges, wharves, embankments and tunnels were constructed, channels
were dredged, and all using manual labour. Workmen soon discovered a

ready market for the artefacts they unearthed and Bronze Age, Iron Age and Roman objects found during this heyday went on to form core parts of the British Museum and the (now) Museum of London's collections. Noël Hume estimates that 90 per cent of the Museum of London's great finds came from labourers during this period. That left 10 per cent from the traditional mudlark. And when work became mechanised, when piles began to be drilled instead of foundations dug, when the great engineering projects tailed off, the opportunity for that thrill of important discovery quickly diminished.

Talking to contemporary archaeologists can make the river seem bounteous again. Over a coffee in Leather Lane, around the corner from the offices of Historic England, Jane Sidell, Inspector of Ancient Monuments for everything under high tide, described the river in terms of Bronze and Iron Age settlements. She mentioned the 3,500-year-old skull found in Chelsea giving evidence of early neurosurgery, as well as uncountable Bronze Age swords. But for Jane, the number of swords is not just a boon for research, it is a rather shameful show of conspicuous consumption by people whom agricultural and technological booms had given a surplus, and who (possibly) demonstrated it by ostentatiously throwing brand new and expensive swords into the river. The Bronze Age was a fall from innocence from which we have never recovered. Looking at the oligarchic wealth currently piled up in London it's possible to observe a continuum. But swords and skulls are not my experience of mudlarking; they are not common finds along the river. I find small things: pieces of broken pottery, a bottle here and there, and metalwork like pins and buttons. Some people find ancient coins, but I don't. I seem to have coin blindness: a button, the same size and shape, I can spot metres away. I tell myself that I don't want to find coins, I never liked them anyway, but I know it's not true. My rationale is that pottery (a warm and human material) and costumes were made for people to admire. They were objects to be owned, and kept, perhaps even passed on through generations. But coins are only ever minted to be exchanged, swapped for something better, something permanent. So I think it is okay that I don't find coins; I am finding what they were made to buy.

For a long time, archaeologists saw only limited value in such less-spectacular finds from the Thames, because they were almost always found out of context. This means they weren't found in an orderly stratigraphy, with the most recent layers on top, and the oldest at the bottom. For the majority of the twentieth century, archaeologists were interested in small objects only in so far as they helped date layers of structures. Because the surface of the Thames foreshore has been so thoroughly muddled by the action of the river, such finds were of little interest.

This has changed, in part thanks to the Portable Antiquities Scheme (PAS). The PAS was introduced across England and Wales towards the end of the last century and is well known to anyone who searches for artefacts, whether they mudlark or metal detect. Anything interesting discovered by an amateur ought to be reported to the PAS, where it will be assessed and recorded. In under twenty years it has become an extraordinary record of the nation's heritage, an online database of over a million finds from across the country. When I spoke to Michael Lewis, the head of the PAS, he explained that archaeologists have come to realise that with enough data points, small objects can provide huge amounts of information. This means the PAS has become a goldmine for archaeologists, giving them insight into the distribution of objects and culture and bringing about the discovery of new sites. The PAS has been so successful in bridging the resource of the amateur and the expertise of the professional that other countries now look to England as a case study in how to get it right.

While we were talking about walking by the river, Michael also said something very interesting. We were discussing the way we felt ill-at-ease each time we crossed the boundary from the path to the foreshore. It is illicit; every stimulus tells you that you're doing something you shouldn't.

'I seem to have coin blindness: a button, the same size and shape, I can spot metres away. I tell myself that I don't want to find coins, I never liked them anyway, but I know it's not true.'

Michael said, 'It's not London,' and I realised that everyone I'd spoken to about being on the foreshore had said something similar. Being on the foreshore of the Thames feels completely separate from the contemporary city. In part this is, I think, a response to the natural environment, to the tides that typically fill the river basin. It is a place that does not exist for Londoners for twelve hours a day, inundated, completely covered by the vastness of the river. I hadn't even realised the waters of the Thames ebbed away until I saw Mark Dion's *Tate Thames Dig*, a giant cabinet of river finds, in its installation at Tate Modern in the early-2000s. To enter the intertidal zone (a space uncannily like the Zone, the industrial wasteland in Andrei Tarkovsky's film *Stalker*) is to enter a truly hidden space. It is also a human response; on the beach you are alone, exposed, never quite sure whether it's legal to be there (it is); and moreover, you are displaced in time. Modernity doesn't exist on the foreshore. It is the one place where ancient litter outnumbers the contemporary. It is empty, derelict, rotting. There is history, but there is also the future, the future of *After London*, Richard Jefferies' Victorian post-apocalyptic melodrama, with its vision of oozing black swamps covering the city. Underfoot, Jefferies' prediction holds true. The thick black mud has already swallowed his London, occasionally spitting it out again.

But not as often as it used to. In 1956, Noël Hume wrote that six years previously it had been 'possible to walk along the shore and expect to

'You are displaced in time. Modernity doesn't exist on the foreshore. It is the one place where ancient litter outnumbers the contemporary. It is empty, derelict, rotting. There is history, but there is also future.'

find at least fifteen or twenty objects that were worth retaining'. As he wrote, however, he would 'go over that ground half a dozen times and find nothing'. He blamed the days after the end of the Second World War, when the 'river's trinket box was opened virtually for the first time, and everything that could readily be seen was taken by the many mudlarks who foraged *en masse*'.

I think the trinket box still holds treasure enough. Perhaps great finds are less frequent, but even bringing home a fragment of mediæval pottery is enough to conjure real romance for the amateur. And, to me, that is what is most beautiful about the River Thames and its periodic foreshore. It is, to take the title of the wonderful book by Stephen Croad, *Liquid History*. What's more, it is the *people's* history, by which I mean that it is a history of individuals, and it is there to be found by everyone. For all the licences required to dig on the foreshore, anyone can walk down to almost any of the beaches at low tide and pick up loose-lying material. It is because of this democratisation of history that I love mudlarking so, and feel that it is of such importance to this city. It is a history of Londoners for Londoners: lost possessions, found again. No equipment required, just a sunny afternoon and a low tide and what was theirs can be yours. I have pieces of glass that I rub like an amulet, pottery with fingerprints that I rest my own inside and feel the walls of history tumble.

This book is an attempt to express that – to make accessible personal histories of London. I am not a professional archaeologist; if anything, I'm closer to those eighteenth-century dilettante antiquarians who have the reputation of magpies. But the River Thames in some ways demands that. It is not a nicely stratified archaeological site. It presents treasures, but with a delightful serendipity; it gives up a hundred random objects, and it is up to the finder to discover their stories. That is the joy of mudlarking: that after every trip to the river you know more than you did before. Chance connections with something that was once treasured, that was once lost and has now been found again. Even the meanest broken fragment tells a story of this great city.

JOURNEYS

Nothing is easier for a man who has, as the phrase goes, 'followed the sea' with reverence and affection, than to evoke the great spirit of the past upon the lower reaches of the Thames. The tidal current runs to and fro in its unceasing service, crowded with memories of men and ships it had borne to the rest of home or to the battles of the sea. It had known and served all the men of whom the nation is proud, from Sir Francis Drake to Sir John Franklin, knights all, titled and untitled – the great knights-errant of the sea. It had borne all the ships whose names are like jewels flashing in the night of time, from the Golden Hind *returning with her rotund flanks full of treasure, to be visited by the Queen's Highness and thus pass out of the gigantic tale, to the* Erebus *and* Terror, *bound on other conquests – and that never returned. It had known the ships and the men. They had sailed from Deptford, from Greenwich, from Erith – the adventurers and the settlers; kings' ships and the ships of men on 'Change; captains, admirals, the dark 'interlopers' of the Eastern trade, and the commissioned 'generals' of East India fleets.*

Joseph Conrad, Heart of Darkness

The river is the history of London. It contains all, reveals all, hides all. 'Light came out of the river', Conrad wrote, in his book that exposed the blackness of it all. Without the Thames there would be no London. The geography and tidal flow gave the Romans what they needed to start their trading centre. Before them, there was no great settlement, only passing peoples, often at war.

But when we walk the banks of the river, collecting what we find, it is clear that the river is no respecter of chronology. Roman is mixed up with Victorian, Mesolithic with contemporary, sometimes the same objects lie side by side, only the date of their creation separating them by thousands of years. The churn of the waters, day after day after day, disperses the old among the new, and the new among the old. I have done the same with this book. To do otherwise would be to misinterpret the Thames. There is nothing linear about this old meandering river.

Instead, I have arranged my finds thematically, looking for common ground across the centuries. Human appetites don't change so very much: our hunger for pleasure, comfort, food itself. Ornaments change; that we feel the need for decoration does not. This first chapter starts with the River Thames and the journeys it inspires. It is the mother of our world: from the river was birthed the city and countless ships sailing on to war, trade, conquest and discovery (and receiving all of these, and more, from others).

'The river is the history of London. It contains all, reveals all, hides all. "Light came out of the river", Conrad wrote, in his book that exposed the blackness of it all. Without the Thames there would be no London.'

I see all of these journeys as central to the London we live in today. They take in not just travel but also the passage of time – through geology and early man to the present day – and of ideas, those intangible things that spring from place to place and settle where minds are fertile. The concept of trading, in particular, affected London's development most of all, filling the river with so varied a collection of artefacts.

Until the Romans, there was no London, but the landscape was inhabited by early humans for about 800,000 years. Throughout the ice ages, they were locked in a battle with encroaching glaciers, colonising and re-colonising as the ice pushed them south. London was never swallowed (the closest the ice came was 430,000 years ago when glaciers pushed as far south as Finchley), but even south of the ice sheet the land was an uninhabitably barren tundra.

In between ice ages, megafauna dominated the landscape. George Monbiot writes about the Victorian excavation of Trafalgar Square revealing masses of bones, of hippopotami, elephants, aurochs and lions. He ties this to a theory that our native plant-life evolved to defend itself against these giant beasts, particularly the straight-tusked elephant, *Elephas antiquus*, that the reason low trees like box and holly and yew are so tough, and grow back so ferociously, is to withstand the predations of the beasts. The mechanism that lets us lay a hedge (slashing the trunk so that the crown hangs on by a thread, only for it to regrow next season tougher than ever) comes from the recovery of an elephant-trampled tree.

Britain was connected by land bridges to Ireland and Europe. The vast area now under the North Sea, called Doggerland, is to me one of the most romantic of lost lands, more so even than Atlantis. It is wonderful to think, sailing from Harwich to the Hook of Holland, that the ferry passes less than a hundred metres above what was once a rich prairie, teaming with life.

Around 10,000 years ago, when the climate improved, human cultures returned for good. Flint tools from the Mesolithic and the Neolithic are found along the river. One flake from the border between the two is illustrated on pages 30–1. Britain was on the outskirts of the great populations of Europe, but ideas and fashions spread here with trade and invasions. Cultural and technological innovations continue to bubble here as in a crucible (see pages 158–9), simmering until something remarkable bursts out.

The journey of the city of London truly begins with the Romans. Julius Caesar had made two attempts to conquer Britain in 55 and 54 BC, but the

Romans did not successfully establish themselves for another hundred years, when the Emperor Claudius invaded in AD 43. They landed in Kent (home of the famous English oysters, see pages 114–15) and settled on the site of the present City. The location of Londinium, a dip in the landscape by a great tidal river, was strategically perfect: a point easily reached from the sea yet right at the heart of the new Roman province, Britannia. It is astonishing to look at plans that recreate the land two thousand years ago. The north bank appears much the same as today (Bazalgette has changed it a little, but it's a recognisable river bank). The south shore wasn't even land. It was islands of marsh and swamp floating in gigantic mud flats. There are still hints of that in Lambeth street names; Lower Marsh, for example, was a road cut through the southern bogs.

The site was economically strategic too. London was well-placed within the country to allow a neutral body (if an invading force can be called that) to trade fairly with warring British tribes. Tribes that were unable to trust each other could trust the Roman middle-man. Though blood-feuds and rotten histories prevented them from meeting one another, they could buy each other's goods *via* Roman intermediaries.

In this way, London has not changed so very much in two thousand years. The City, 'Change, as Conrad refers to it, stands, supposedly neutral, the spider at the centre of the web of the global free market. Markets, the idea behind the City, were imported, initiated by the Roman invader, adapted, improved upon, made world-dominating. And still fiercely defended, though many in the country doubt the necessity of aligning our interests so closely with those of finance.

Britain was late to the party. A late addition to the Roman Empire, late to begin her own. We can think today of the British Empire as supreme, catastrophic perhaps for both the colonised and the colonisers. Yet Britain's empire was hardly the first, has not proven to be the last. Tribes war, conquer, enslave. China lay at the centre of the world long before the Roman Empire. As Europe emerged from the Middle Ages, Portugal and Spain (themselves emerging from Moorish rule) had effectively divided the profitable new world between them, stripping it of precious metals, ever-searching for El Dorado. England looked on enviously.

The entry into empire began as pirates, free-loaders, buccaneers. The most famous Elizabethan sailors are those who ransacked Spanish riches. Sir Frances Drake and Sir Walter Raleigh, our national heroes, were lords of plunder. Coming from behind, the English began to overtake. Imported technologies were improved: the study of navigation; even naval firepower, with foreign brass cannon translated into vastly cheaper English iron ones. And perhaps most important of all, stolen riches were reinvested: first of all in sugar and tobacco plantations. The hunt for Inca gold was transformed into practical farming. This holds the darkness at the heart of all stories of the Empire, the slavery on which the city is built. Of course, Joseph Conrad was writing about the cruelty of the Belgian Empire, cruelty that made even the British blanch.

London became the centre of the trade in new world goods. Sugar, tobacco, tea, coffee and chintzes poured up the River Thames and were sold on again to European buyers. War with the Dutch made possible the East India Company (it is incredible to me that the Dutch Navy sailed up the Thames in relatively recent history, Pepys' anguished diarising shows the English of the day were just as surprised, 'All our hearts do now ake; for the newes is true, that the Dutch have broke the chaine and burned our ships'). The Dutch got spice, the English textiles, and with them the rule of India.

At any point on this journey it could appear the path to Empire was predetermined, even divine. But nothing was inevitable for this Island Nation. Britain's history was made by individuals, some famous, most not: for example, without Samuel Pepys' improvements to the Navy, dreams of the Empire might have been long forgotten. Yet separated from Europe since Doggerland had been flooded by a mega-tsunami in 6000 BC, isolation had given Britons a hard-headed mind for trade and a willingness to make anyone a commercial partner.

Many of the objects in this book, not just in this chapter, came to London through trade. Pottery from Italy, glass from Germany, pins from France. Others come through immigration: the delftware potters came from Antwerp, settling first in Norfolk before colonising the Thames. Their iconic blue-and-white was modelled on Chinese fashion, at the same time as blue-and-white Chinese porcelains were being exported to London *via* Portugal. Pipes smoked imported tobacco. Teapots brewed imported tea. London is an *entrepôt*, a nation of shopkeepers, and everything that came here or went out again passed over the River Thames. All these finds start with that journey.

FOSSIL SEA URCHIN

Conulus spp.
Late Cretaceous (80–65 million years ago)

The artefacts open with a fossil sea urchin, not because it's the oldest object that I've found, but because it bridges the natural and human London: alive 80 million years ago, slowly turned into flint, then found again and judged precious. This was found in a spot of known Mesolithic activity. Fossil sea urchins such as this have been treasured, worked, buried with *Homo* species for hundreds of thousands of years.

When this sea urchin was alive, most of the British Isles sat underneath a narrow sea between North America and Europe. This island has been submerged many times in its geological history. Each submersion adds a layer to the strata of rocks around us. The Cretaceous is marked by great chalk layers – famous in the white cliffs – formed of the skeletons of innumerable tiny sea creatures. Fixed within the pure white are fossils of larger sealife, some of them chalky, some of them nodules of flint like this one. The London Basin (the lowlands lying between the Chilterns and the North Downs from Wiltshire to the sea) sits on this chalk. In places, it is exposed, and flints and fossils (and flint fossils) erode out and are discovered.

Fossil sea urchins have been found in England in graves from 2000 BC, underneath houses built in AD 400, at the centre of a 400,000-year-old flint axe. They're the fairy's stone, Fairy Loafs and Shepherd's Crowns. They're found collected by humans and our predecessors throughout Europe, Asia and Africa. They are the original five-pointed star, transposed into art ancient and modern. This fossil represents our capacity for metaphor, for mystical thinking, for the unquenchable desire to collect.

And it also speaks to me of the impermanence of our comfortable world. If London was once at the bottom of the seas, then when will that happen again? What will the city look like at the cusp of that geological calamity? Who will live here? Will it be a thriving megalopolis like today, except more so, serviced by an AI economy, traversed by hoverboards? Or will it resemble the Neolithic past, populated by cliff-dwelling tribes sharing hulking concrete precipices with guillemots and kittiwakes?

This book is a story of everyday objects, items too quotidian to have attracted any real consideration in their day. And yet because of that, because they were created, broken, thrown away without a thought for future, they make me think, just like this sea urchin makes me think, that all things will pass away, so what are the fossils that we will leave behind?

I saw a modern knife, maybe 1980s, of the sort that might have been disposed of in a hurry. When I bent down to pick it up, Sara, with whom I'd come to the foreshore because she knew about flint tools, picked up the stone lying next to it. It was a beautiful, perfect blade, Mesolithic, from the Stone Age. It is impossible to convey the stab of jealousy one feels at a moment like that. Of course I was overjoyed at her find, I said, while I stared daggers at my feet. And there, right by my boots, was this, tiny in comparison but exquisite. A flake of flint from the period where the Mesolithic ended and the Neolithic began, between 6000 and 4000 BC.

It's undoubtably worked, but it's not so certain it was ever used. It comes from the manufacture of a larger flint tool, a knife or axe, but it's so elegant and sharp that I'd be surprised if a Stone Age craftsman hadn't put it to some purpose. Microliths, smaller flakes of this shape, were used as the points on fishing spears, or as their barbs. Mesolithic spears had more than one flint blade attached to make certain that the fish didn't slip off. This one is still frighteningly sharp, needle-like, and faceted like a jewel. It's jewel-like too, so fine as to be translucent. I could well imagine it pointing up a spear.

Finding it lessened my envy somewhat and I gave my eighties knife to Sara. She held the two blades together, weighty, one in each hand. Maybe both had been used for the same murderous purpose, separated by six thousand years. The Thames can do that, throw up confluences of time. Maybe, just maybe, something of the modern knife would have survived a few thousand years into the future, if it came to be embedded deep in the anoxic mud. It would probably carry enough twentieth-century air inside the case to rust itself into an unrecognisable lump. Ferrous metals don't last long by the Thames. But flint tools will still be identifiable come the next geological age, embedded in the stratum left behind by the Anthropocene, that thin boundary between the Cenozoic and whatever's coming next.

FLINT FLAKE

Possibly used in a fishing spear
Around 6000–4000 BC

Made by Dunn Bennet, Burslem, Staffordshire
1896–1904

At the time of writing, the Japanese company NYK is the fourteenth largest shipping company in the world. Its combined ships could carry half a million containers at once.

At the turn of the last century, when this piece of pottery was made, NYK had broken through a European cartel to become the first Asian company to ship from London to the East. NYK was born of an 1885 government mandated merger between Mitsubishi (yes, that Mitsubishi, then known as the Mitsubishi Mail Steamship Company) and a rival whom the Japanese government had set up three years earlier to temper Mitsubishi's dominance. The competition almost bankrupted them both, hence rapid bandaging together.

NYK's international routes came about when they and Tata & Sons (yes, that Tata, owner of Jaguar Land Rover) got together to break the monopoly P&O had in exporting cotton from Bombay to Japan. NYK battled P&O again when they set up their London line – initially being only permitted to offload in London but having to steam up to Middlesborough (*via* Antwerp) to load freight for Japan. The European–Far East Conference, which tried to stop NYK's entry to the UK, was essentially a collusion between shipping companies to blockade their home ports and 'manage' prices; which is not entirely to paint NYK as the underdog. They were heavily subsidised by the Japanese Government with money paid by the losing side of the Sino-Japanese war (China was the losing side). In 1899 full service began, to London and back again.

This seems to encapsulate the docks of London, if not the city as a whole. The docks were truly a global microcosm, spilling over with goods and people from most every country. As he toured the city with Gustave Doré in the 1870s, William Blanchard Jerrold describes the kaleidoscope of the docks as 'black with coal, blue with indigo, brown with hides, white with flour; stained with purple wine–or brown with tobacco'. Yet for all their internationalism, they were also fiercely protectionist: imports and exports were here for the profit of our businessmen (though certainly not for the dockers, the stevedores, the longshoremen). Today, as Patrick Keiller returns to repeatedly in *Robinson in Space*, ownership of ports is foreign and opaque. The new owners see memories of culture and traditions 'as impediments to development'. This Staffordshire plate dates from between 1896 and 1904, after which NYK started using Japanese ceramics.

This is not the Southern Railway that, according to the Daily Mail, receives 5,000 angry tweets a day. This is the Southern Railway that served its passengers tea in china cups as they rattled along towards Padstow or Plymouth. The difference is a story of fifty years and a swinging pendulum of regulation.

The Southern Railway with the crockery was set up in 1923, the year of the Great Grouping. Britain's railways had been constructed by speculators, rogues and geniuses. The coming of trains had transformed the economy, geography and landscape of the country and supercharged the Industrial Revolution. Railways spread like miasma. Around new stations, towns would spontaneously generate. But the lines were incredibly inefficient. Rampant competition between the hundred-plus railway companies had led to routes that were duplicated, or stopped dead at the boundaries between rival territories.

In the First World War, the government took control. The State ran the railways well. They rationalised things. I don't know if they made the trains run on time, but I have my suspicions. After the War, the State kept hold until 1921; as they prepared to release the trains back into private hands the government was determined not to lose all that had been gained. They passed the Railways Act 1921. Hence the Grouping.

The hundred companies became four: Southern; Great Western; London, Midland and Scottish; and London and North Eastern. More than twenty companies were merged to make the Southern Railway. Headquartered in Waterloo and sending passengers on trains like the Night Ferry and the Devon Belle, the Southern Railway was the most popular of the Big Four. Their exquisite posters appealed to both the cosmopolitan, with the Atlantic Coast Express ('Cross the Atlantic by White Star') and the homebodies ('Live in Kent and be Content'). The green of this teacup matches the green of the new engines the company invested in.

The Big Four ran on empty throughout the Second World War. They kept the country moving but were exhausted by the effort, and when the War ended they were almost bankrupt. In 1947 Clement Attlee's government passed another major Act, and all lines came together at last. British Railways was born. In 1997, the railway was privatised once more.

Southern Railway South Western Section
1923–47

PALACE OF WESTMINSTER MASONRY BLOCK

Spandrel fragment from the Old Palace of
Westminster
Sixteenth or seventeenth century

The journey of this masonry has been more eventful than most. It hasn't travelled far, but before sinking into the Thames it was burnt, buried and then blown up. Now fallen, it was once mighty, a giant fragment from a window of the old Palace of Westminster, carved in the sixteenth or seventeenth century.

It's a beautiful piece of stone: shield-shaped with curling strapwork reminiscent of an unfurling fern. And heavy, too. Seventeen kilograms, half a metre long, a quarter deep. I didn't want to carry it home, but I didn't want to leave it behind. It fit in my knapsack, just, and I lugged it away.

Later, I was introduced to James Wright of Museum of London Archaeology, and he recognised the very piece. He'd recorded it in an archaeological survey of foreshore fragments from Victoria Tower Gardens, it was part of a spandrel from the palace window tracery. Spandrels are the two triangles of wall above an archway; I've loved the word since encountering it in an argument between Stephen Jay Gould and Daniel Dennett over whether it was a useful term to use in evolutionary theory.

So this spandrel fragment came from above a window of the old Palace of Westminster, and returned to earth when the Palace burned down in 1834. What began as a chimney fire, started by burning the Exchequer's tally sticks, spread slowly, and then exploded in the early evening. Thick crowds gathered to watch the judgement on the Poor Law Bill (said Thomas Carlyle). Turner produced two fine pictures from sketches he made on the south bank. His colour harmonies would later inspire the Impressionists.

The palace rubble was reused fifty years later, to back-fill the expanded embankment that makes up Victoria Tower Gardens. This spandrel became nothing more than hardcore. Then, on 16 March 1941, a German bomb hit the river wall, blasting the buried rubble into the Thames. A concrete scar still marks the site where the wall was fissured, still traceable like Doris Salcedo's *Shibboleth*, whose rupture, now filled and polished but visible all the same, runs across the floor of the Turbine Hall in the Tate Modern. For over sixty years the carved masonry sat on the foreshore, until I came along. A little while after I first wrote to him, James emailed me back. 'The best thing to do', he wrote, 'is to redeposit it as close to the find spot as you can.' I looked balefully at my knapsack.

These words are from a publication by the American Tract Society, *The Pictorial Tract Primer*. In full they would have read:

> X is the CROSS,
> That our dear Saviour bore:
> O think of his Sorrows,
> And grieve him no more.

The Pictorial Tract Primer was more than just an alphabet in picture and Christian verse. It was also a vocabulary; a grammar; a series on natural history ('Here is a Lamb. Does it not put you in mind of the Lamb of God who did no sin . . . ?'); it contained poetry and lessons from the Bible.

What was a verse from an American book doing on an English cup? In the early-eighteenth century, great religious movements began to form around charismatic leaders. Preachers held vast audiences captive with their fiery oratory on the plains and hillsides of Britain. It was the period when John Wesley founded Methodism. There were liberal and illiberal teachings (some preachers favoured child labour, but from these evangelicals also came the missionaries campaigning against slavery). In 1799 the movement birthed the Religious Tract Society of London, with the aim of 'converting, sanctifying, and comforting souls'.

By any measure, the Tract Society was successful. In its own reckoning it 'assailed popery on the Continent of Europe, Mohammedanism in the East, and paganism of various forms in heathen lands. . . . Its publications have passed the wall of China, and have entered the palace of the Celestial emperor.' In its first fifty years it had circulated 500 million tracts.

The American Tract Society formed in 1825. This illustrated primer is just one of their weapons of God. Perhaps they commissioned this cup from a Staffordshire pottery, and it was lost en route back to America.

There is some truth in the Marxist argument that evangelicalism held the working classes in their places; at the very least it was a good partner to industrial capitalism. But, as this fragment shows, one of the great tools of the evangelical was education. Until 1967, the Religious Tract Society was still publishing *The Boy's Own Paper*.

Mid- to late-nineteenth century

WEDGE AND BRASS SHEETING

Possibly from the construction of the
SS *Great Eastern*
1854–7

I was looking at a spot washed clear of gravel at the tip of the Isle of Dogs. Sometimes the eddies of the water or the shape of the land change the texture of the beach in just a small area; the same processes seem to deposit finds. It's worth standing over one a while. I heard someone calling me. It wasn't my friend Nic, with whom I'd come; it was a man at the tideline, which I'd written off as treacherous mud. I asked him if he was all right. He said he'd found something I should see.

If he could walk there, so could I; I tip-toed over and he held out some brass nails, Tudor, possibly. Then he looked down at a puddle where there were three more and said they were mine. Beautiful golden brass, like rivets but rounded and sharply spiked. He introduced himself as Peter. We walked together.

Peter came to this beach on the Isle of Dogs every day when he could. Twice a day if the tides both fell in daylight. There was a ladder that he liked to use (Nic and I had come from Johnson's Drawdock, to the east, and walked laboriously over shattered black cobbles). He showed me some of his recent finds on his phone. A mediæval comb, almost perfect; a solid gold locket, heart-shaped, engraved with rococo lines. But he also mudlarked for what was practical; coal for a mate, lead for scrap, brass nails were upcycled, used to make period restorations perfect. He'd even found his bicycle in the river.

We came to another glint of brass. A sheet. It was where Isambard Kingdom Brunel had the SS *Great Eastern* made. The leviathan (indeed SS *Leviathan* was the name she was first given) was the largest ship ever built. There was no larger ship made until the final year of the nineteenth century. Thousands of men took four years to build her. Two gigantic paddle wheels extended from her side. About 3 million rivets held the hull together.

Nearby was a portion of the slipway from which the *Great Eastern* had been launched (in 1858, on the fourth attempt, three months after the first). She lasted only thirty years. Unsuccessful as a cargo vessel, she laid cable between Britain and the US and was scrapped in Liverpool in 1889. Her top mast became the Liverpool Football Club flagpole.

A few metres further on I found a wedge. 'I found a tool around here,' Peter said, 'marked IB.'

London was occupied by the Romans for nearly four hundred years, from AD 47 to some point in the 400s. That's at least as long as from today to the Great Fire of London. It's a staggering length of time, and therefore not surprising that there are so many Roman artefacts to be found.

I've included this Roman flagon in my section on Journeys not because it travelled from Rome (it's much more likely to have been made in England) but because it represents the overwhelming, country-defining power of the journey of ideas: of technology, commercial systems and political will.

Before the Romans brought Britain into their empire, Julius Caesar wrote that its inhabitants 'live on milk and meat, and wear skins. All the Britons dye their bodies with woad, which produces a blue colour, and this gives them a more terrifying appearance in battle'. The only civilised parts of the country, he thought, were the harbours of Kent. But in just ten years after they successfully conquered the country, the Romans had created of London a prosperous, built-up centre.

In AD 60, just as things appeared settled, a rebel army under Boudica burned the city flat. Underground, a red layer of ash almost two thousand years old marks the moment of that insurgent whirlwind. After a retributory slaughtering of Boudica's Iceni (Tacitus quotes 80,000 Britons put to the sword) London was remade into a perfect Roman green zone.

Where does the flagon fit into this? It shows that for all the blood spilled, the Roman colonisation was won with soft power, not hard. Britain became Romanised because the Romans brought something better than woad. This flagon probably held wine produced in an English vineyard. It was the Romans who brought this agricultural knowledge. There's a business theory called the Kano Model that states that customer satisfaction is less related to the basic service than to insignificant extras that satisfy subconscious desires: a crèche at IKEA or kids' smoothies at the sofa.com showroom. I think it applies to cultural imperialism too. It's not just about effective rule: it's who has the best drinks – whether that's Coca-Cola or English wine.

ROMAN FLAGON BOTTOM

AD 100–200

BLEU PERSAN DELFTWARE

Possibly Nevers, France
Late-seventeenth century

This white decoration is on an exquisitely rich, dark, cobalt blue background. The few lines left to us could be absolutely anything, but I have a suspicion that it's part of a Chinese gown, and if not a gown, an oriental tree. Here's why.

This fragment is tin-glazed pottery, or delftware. It's quite an unusual style (which is why I picked it up, for all its figural limitations) – a reverse of the much more common blue pattern on a white ground. But is it still delftware? Not exactly, because delftware was being made in London well before it was being made in Delft. That town came late, and became the most famous for it, and to the victor, the spoils.

There's an even better reason why it shouldn't be called delftware, which takes in half the globe at a gallop. Delftware came to London from Flanders (there were potters from Antwerp here during the reign of Queen Elizabeth I – Delft got it from them too, in the end), and it came to Flanders from Urbino in Italy (where it's called maiolica), and it came to Italy from Moorish Spain, and it came to Moorish Spain from the Islamic East, and it came to the Islamic potters from China. A thousand years ago or more.

This piece confounds that lineage, a little bit. Because the idea for white on blue didn't come to England from Flanders; it came from Nevers, in France (where incidentally we call tin-glazed pottery faience). The Neverites, around 1650, created this exquisite style called *bleu persan* (from the Persians) and they almost always decorated it with Chinese motifs, like figures in verdant settings. So that's why I think these lines are almost certainly a gown. But if they're not, then they're definitely an oriental tree.

If this sounds too simple, well, perhaps. Delftware potters communicated across countries: many were from the same families. Around the same time *bleu persan* came out of Nevers, it was also being discovered in Flanders and London. But like Delft and delftware, with *bleu persan* Nevers gets the credit and the spoils.

FIGURES AND FLOWERS

PORCELAIN
WITH ANGOULÊME
SPRIGS
1790 — 1810

Have nothing in your house that you do not know to be useful or believe to be beautiful.' So wrote William Morris. The following fragments certainly aren't useful and they're not necessarily all that interesting. But what they are is beautiful. This is why I go mudlarking. For all the deep experiences of history, that just-tangible connection to the Londoners who last held the objects I find, my mudlarking is primarily aesthetic. Perhaps that's what marks me as the eternal amateur.

At some point in the life-history of rubbish it changes from trash to treasure. It passes through some lens and becomes a valued artefact. Is it scarcity? A distance from memory? Perhaps it is the reassurance that two hundred years from now future humans will look at our detritus with something other than the disgust with which we view it now. When all the plastic landfills have been mined for their hydrocarbon chains, someone will hold one half of an IKEA saucer and admire its broken Scandinavian patterns. That is what these objects are. They are in the river because someone didn't want them enough. But being found, they have been brought back to life. I want them.

More than anything I love having these around. I love to look at them. To admire their brush strokes, their depictions, their colours. I love the richness of their tones. I like to hold them, to feel their weight or their weightlessness in my hand, their sheens and lustres. I like how some of these are dramatically over-the-top; I particularly love the sense that these are beautiful only in fragment, that a complete object decorated like this would be garish, intrusive, *fusty*. But broken, they are the perfect metaphor for humanity, and that makes them beautiful too.

JAPANESE CRANE PATTERN

Plate by Christopher Dresser, Minton
Around 1880

RUAN PLAYER[*]

Flow blue bowl base
Late-nineteenth century

[*] It's equally possible he's a European
lute player.

COCKEREL

Green transferware, probably Staffordshire
Late-nineteenth century

CHINESE PHEASANT

Overpainted transferware cup
Mid- to late-nineteenth century

IS THERE A COAT OF ARMS IN THIS FLOWER?

One-colour printed pattern with overpainting
Mid- to late-nineteenth century

REMINISCENT OF THE INDIAN TREE PATTERN

One-colour printed pattern with overpainting
Mid- to late-nineteenth century

MAGNOLIA FLOWERS

One-colour printed pattern with overpainting
Mid- to late-nineteenth century

ORIENTAL FLOWERS

Outline printed in puce and overpainted bone
china
Nineteenth century

CORNFLOWER PATTERN

Cornflower pattern, also known as Angoulême
sprigs
Large porcelain cup (exterior)
1790–1810

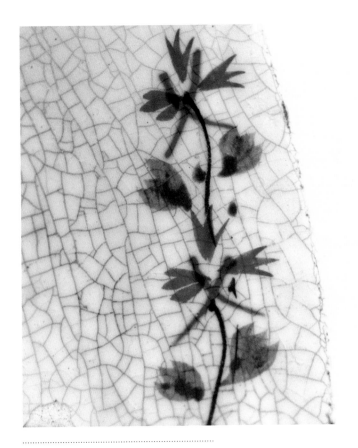

Detail of the Angoulême sprigs
Large porcelain cup (interior)
1790–1810

Angoulême sprigs were pioneered by the
Duc d'Angoulême's porcelain factory in Paris
(founded in 1781). Elegant English were quick
to adopt the motif.

GILDED MOULDED FOLIAGE

Probably the elaborate finial lid of a tureen,
ironstone china
Early- to mid-nineteenth century

Transferware
Nineteenth century

TEDDY BEAR HEAD

Teddy bear head. Unless it's a cat. Or a bear.
Or a dog.
Japan
Twentieth century

WOLF

Bartmann jug armorial medallion
Seventeenth century

If the animal is a lion, then this is likely to be the
coat of arms of Amsterdam. However, I think
it's a wolf. A dog has proven a pretty popular
alternative, and plenty of people think it's a
dragon. Animal fragments are a mystery.

STRAWBERRY PLANT

Detail of strawberry plant
Transferware, ironstone china
Early- to mid-nineteenth century

BILLOWING FLOWERS

Either a Chinese vase with spray of flowers
or a censer with billowing smoke
Delftware saucer dish or bowl
Mid-eighteenth century

TUREEN LID KNOB

Majolica
Mid-nineteenth century

Majolica is quite different from maiolica
with an i. Majolica was a nineteenth-century
recreation of the lovely thick tin-glaze effect
of sixteenth-century maiolica.

WISPY FLOWERS

Enchantingly simple and wispy flowers
One-colour printed pattern with overpainting
Mid- to late-nineteenth century

PLEASURE AND VICE

To me, any serious study of dissipation in London should begin with the deliciously viperish book All the Tea in China, *by Kyril Bonfiglioli. Although not published until 1978, and therefore qualifying for the suspect genre of historical fiction, it remains the truest embodiment of the licentious overindulgence, venal pleasure-seeking and canny, hard-headed, bull-headed merchantising that created the London we know today. Few pre-twentieth century books could have risked being so filthy; the publication of* Fanny Hill *in 1748 resulted in warrants issued for the arrest of the author, publisher and printer. In this introduction I want to celebrate this pleasure in its purest form, through drink, and masses of it. Later, in the artefacts that follow, I will discuss the many undoubted crimes, crimes against humanity even, with which London bought its unrivalled wealth.*

Written by an art dealer of the old school, more famous for his black-comedy thrillers *The Mortdecai Trilogy*, *All the Tea in China* tells how nineteenth-century Carolus Mortdecai Van Cleef made his fortune selling opium and pottery. It is in every way unreconstructed and yet has such force of life as to make every odious slander shimmer. Van Cleef, fleeing a riding-crop wedding in his native Holland, is set up near Covent Garden by a tea merchant, John Jorrocks of Great Corum Street (in constant competition with 'young Charlie Harrod' over who can get the new season's Oolong to market first). As an introduction to the merchant class – so vital to the genesis of today's London – the book is unparalleled. But more, it highlights the critical importance of excess to a Londoner, to an Englishman (and to a Dutchman: there are many similarities between our two histories and cultures, which is why after the trade wars were settled, William of Orange was so gladly welcomed as monarch).

Van Cleef and Jorrocks are two opposing types of merchant, the first a rapier, the other a pudding, and yet both are mavens about their percentum. They favour each other because of what their 'stomicks' hold, and trust comes through competitive consumption, of waistcoat-tightening descriptions of gourmandery and drinking until they've drunk themselves sober.

Jorrocks is a loveable kitten, the ur-Cockaigne. But Bonfiglioli stole him wholesale, name, accents and appetites, from the early-nineteenth-century stories by Robert Smith Surtees, incredibly popular sporting tales that

'They favour each other because of what their "stomicks" hold, and trust comes through competitive consumption, of waistcoat-tightening descriptions of gourmandery and drinking until they've drunk themselves sober.'

dominated the way in which the hunting city gent was seen throughout the Victorian period. Surtees' Jorrocks is the true depiction of the self-made Londoner, the bedrock of the city. For this merchant prince, every meal of the day was his most important meal; breakfast was 'a magnificent uncut ham, with a great quartern loaf on one side and a huge Bologna sausage on the other; besides these there were nine eggs, two pyramids of muffins, a great deal of toast, a dozen ship-biscuits, and half a pork-pie, while a dozen kidneys were spluttering on a spit before the fire, and Betsy held a gridiron covered with mutton-chops on the top . . .'. Wittles for a woyage were 'a knuckle of weal, half a ham, beef, sarsingers, chickens, sherry white . . .'; and when hungry in Paris he asks to be granted

> . . . but one request, and that is the contents of a single sentence.
> 'I want a roasted or boiled leg of mutton, beef, hung beef, a quarter of mutton, mutton chops, veal cutlets, stuffed tongue, dried tongue, hog's pudding, white sausage, meat sausage, chicken with rice, a nice fat roast fowl, roast chicken with cressy, roast or boiled pigeon, a fricassee of chicken, sweet-bread, goose, lamb, calf's cheek, calf's head, fresh pork, salt meat, cold meat, hash.'

Everything is accompanied by eye-watering quantities of ardent spirits, from gallons of brandy and water to 'a large black bottle of Hollands, labelled "Eye Water," part of a contraband cargo'. Jorrocks was appropriated widely, his unquenchable appetites just too delicious to leave alone. He arose at the same time as that other joyous imbiber and inspiration, Charles Dickens' early character, Mr Pickwick.

I prefer discussing brazen pleasures in this introduction and will postpone the sanctimony of vice until we look at the objects. For the same reason, I have always preferred the *joie de vivre* of Mr Pickwick to Dickens' later, undoubtedly better, more altogether troubling novels. It is not so much drowning *my* sorrows, as drowning the world's.

With Mr Pickwick, as with Jorrocks, serious, dedicated, drinking is often ritualised. Performed in a group of close friends, accompanied by speeches, toasts and song. Participants know what to say, how to react, which oath to pledge and the right drink to be drunk. The volume consumed is incredible, but it is a rule-based activity. Today such observances are reserved for weddings or such dining clubs as may involve pigs' heads. But Mr Pickwick knows the purpose of ceremony. It keeps everybody drinking. Picnicking beneath an oak tree, he takes

> . . . another glass to the health of their absent friend, and then felt himself imperatively called upon to propose another in honour of the punch-compounder, unknown.
>
> This constant succession of glasses produced considerable effect upon Mr. Pickwick; his countenance beamed with the most sunny smiles, laughter played around his lips, and good-humoured merriment twinkled in his eye. Yielding by degrees to the influence of the exciting liquid, rendered more so by the heat, Mr. Pickwick expressed a strong desire to recollect a song which he had heard in his infancy, and the attempt proving abortive, sought to stimulate his memory with more glasses of punch, which appeared to have quite a contrary effect; for, from forgetting the words of the song, he began to forget how to articulate any words at all; and finally, after rising to his legs to address the company in an eloquent speech, he fell into the barrow, and fast asleep, simultaneously.

Where did these Falstaffian drunkards come from? Well, in part from Falstaff, the most notorious of all the besozzled. And before him, from Chaucer and his soul of England (and born entirely of London). *The Canterbury Tales* fits perfectly into the myth of Merrie England, in many ways propagates it, but it does so at the exclusion of the lowest in society. The Tabard, the inn at the centre of the *Tales*, is a genteel place. Although set amongst the Southwark stews, it is determinedly not an ale-house: a category of establishment where whores and cut-purses were found. Falstaff's spiritual home, The Boar's-Head Tavern, Eastcheap, was decidedly lower rent. There Mistress Quickly so well supplies Sir John that he can be described with the rhetorical questioning of 'Can a weak empty vessel bear such a huge full hogshead? There's a whole merchant's venture of Bourdeaux stuff in him; you have not seen a hulk better stuffed in the hold . . .'

Falstaff was England's greatest drinker, but he was written mourning an end of the lowest class of merriment, for merriment is only truly merry when it flirts with the gutter. When Hal threw Falstaff aside in *Henry* IV, *Part 2* it marked a long winter for the English drinker. Shakespeare wrote under a political and religious crackdown. Protestant coldness had replaced the genial warmth of Chaucer's England, and taverns and ale-houses were suffering. (Inns, being higher-status, weathered this storm. They were meeting places for merchants. They made possible travel along dangerous roads. They facilitated trade.) In writing Falstaff, Shakespeare was looking back at a drunkener England of two centuries earlier.

There were ways around this frigidity. Elizabethan wits found they could elevate their intoxication. As the Renaissance swung belatedly into England, it became a mark of great sophistication to look to classical poets and their liquid inspiration. Drinking in company to make poetry was a fine development. Ben Jonson, in his poem 'Inviting a Friend to Supper' of around 1616, looks forward to the delicious, immortal thoughts they will share, inspired as were the Greeks and Romans:

> . . . a pure cup of rich *Canary*-wine.
> Which is the *Mermaids*, now, but shall be mine:
> Of which had Horace, or Anacreon tasted . . .

The Mermaid was his favourite tavern.

It's interesting here to compare for a moment the figure in the flow blue dish on page 51. This Chinese character probably plays a ruan, named after the famous musician Ruan Xian, who was one of the Seven Worthies of the

'Falstaff was England's greatest drinker, but he was written mourning an end of the lowest class of merriment, for merriment is only truly merry when it flirts with the gutter.'

Bamboo Grove, a drinking club of Taoist philosophers and poets in around AD 200. Deep thought requires deep drinking; another of the Seven Worthies was China's first recorded alcoholic. By the beginning of the seventeenth century, drinking once again came to stand for good company. Not drinking was to be 'branded a Puritan, a Hypocrite, a Precisian', wrote William Prynne in 1628, complaining that drunkenness had been rebranded (to use a modern term), under the 'lovely titles of Hospitality, Good-Fellowship, Courtesy, Entertainment, Joviality, Mirth . . .'. I'd rather be a good-fellow than a precisian, any day. Prynne and the Puritans had their day, of course, and took all the pleasure from Londoners for the duration of the Commonwealth, but what joy there was when Charles II came back full of French ideas for fashions and festivities.

The Restoration is the bridge between Ben Jonson and Jorrocks, crossed with the precise diarising of Samuel Pepys and then the glorious eighteenth century. I salivate as much over the appetites of Pepys, meticulously documented, as I do when reading Surtees. I am not a big man (nor, of course, was Pepys), but I begin to wish my stomach could hold as much as theirs. Pepys drinks, and is drunk. And when he eats! Such constant, glorious sweetmeats. He even writes about food *on* the river: in the great Frost Fair of January 1684, when the Thames froze over, Pepys walks across it, passing booths roasting meat upon the ice. In his hangovers at least I can rival him, as when on the 22 September 1660, he vomits up

'Samuel Johnson not only claimed that a man who was tired of London was tired of life (one can be just a little weary, surely, without heading for the bathtub with a razorblade?), he also wrote that a man (possibly the same man) is never happy "but when he is drunk".'

all breakfast 'by reason of last night's debauch'. In 1664, he meets the above Prynne, the Puritan, and notices that he refuses to drink all healths. The ritual of drinking is ever-present, the necessity of drinking toasts and healths, which match each drinker drink for drink, and so ensure perfect group cohesion.

All the pleasures of intoxication flowered again in England with the Georges, from palaces to rookeries. They lasted until the next wave of puritanism, again from overseas, in the stiff form of Prince Albert. Jorrocks and Pickwick have Georgian appetites, just as Falstaff had Chaucerian. They are a nostalgia for a Golden Age, when John Bull's belly sloshed with beer. The mellow drunken sadness for yesterday is mirrored in literary reflections on it. Oliver Goldsmith sat at The Boar's Head tavern in 1760, 'still kept at East-cheap', and reflected 'Let's have t'other bottle: here's to the memory of Shakespear, Falstaff, and all the merry men.' Samuel Johnson not only claimed that a man who was tired of London was tired of life (one can be just a little weary, surely, without heading for the bathtub with a razorblade?), he also wrote that a man (possibly the same man) is never happy 'but when he is drunk'. I can well imagine the look Johnson would have given a Temperance man from Manchester.

A common theme that runs through the commentary on drinking of a few hundred years ago (and just as much today) is that drunkenness brings harmless and joyful inspiration to the sophisticated wealthy, but is destructive, wasteful and an abomination when practised by the lower orders. It was not alcohol that brought about drunkenness, it was the character of the drinker. The upper classes had control of their temperament, the lower classes did not. They drank because they needed a drink. Life was hard, and they took what pleasure or analgesia from it as they could. And thus, the Gin Craze.

SQUARE GIN BOTTLE BASE

Eighteenth century

London's self-destructive infatuation with gin came and went in a generation, but while it lasted it caused tremendous damage: both to the individual and the body politic. The Gin Craze was ignited by a combination of patriotism, politics and a vicious funnel of economic forces: the growth of the market, and the deflation of costs.

Gin originated in the Netherlands (where it's still sold as jenever), and the taste took off in England in 1688 when the Dutch William of Orange ascended the throne. When wars between England and France made drinking brandy seem traitorous, Parliament gave the loyal nod to gin by deregulating the industry. The result was a bacchanal. Gin consumption rose from half a million gallons in 1688 to 2.5 million in 1720 (at the point the spark really lit the craze) and then to 8.2 million gallons in 1743. To contemporary observers the Gin Craze represented the absolute dissolution of the lower orders.

The most famous depiction is William Hogarth's *Gin Lane*. The counterpoint to it, *Beer Street*'s bullish British wholesomeness, is discussed in the introduction to clay pipes on pages 94–5 . *Gin Lane* is Hogarth's distillation of the political class's gin panic: it shows filicides, suicides and riots, the wanton destruction of a mother's love for her child and the battling Englishman reduced to a skeleton. For a warrior nation, Mother Gin looked set to sap the spirit for good.

Yet Hogarth's picture hints at the causes behind the craze. It loosely portrays St Giles, then a teaming district full of recent migrants from the countryside. In the early-eighteenth century, the price of corn was notably low. This fed the two economic forces: it made gin cheap (almost half of the national wheat harvest was used to make gin in 1750) and it put farm labourers out of work. They travelled to London in great numbers in search of a better life, were packed into degrading tenements by unscrupulous landlords and quickly became the very market that inflamed the Gin Craze. Gin wasn't sold to savour; it was sold to shut out the horrors of the slums.

This calls to mind the distinction Jane Jacobs makes between overcrowding and high densities. Cities need lots of people living together, just not all in the same room. It is vital for cultural and economic life that cities are densely packed, but when every dwelling is abused through a cobweb of sublets all the benefits collapse and what we are left with is Gin Lane.

It's almost impossible to see a wine bottle outside of our modern understanding of their purpose, which is to lie cradled in wine-racks, gently creeping towards drinking age, or to stand in military order, labels vibrantly decorated with examples of Australian humour, across the shelves of our local off licences. And yet when wine bottles were first introduced, and for a century after, such uses were unheard of. Bottles were made, not to keep wine, but to hold it on its journey from the cellar to the table. They were squat, globular, beautiful things, whose primary purpose in design was not to fall over. The changing shape of wine bottles over the next few centuries tells us how international relations changed the taste for wine in England.

The strong green glass bottle was almost certainly the result of detailed research and invention by Sir Kenelm Digby in the early-1630s. Digby was a Catholic, a diplomat, a pirate and a scientist (and mixologist supreme: a future publication demands his recipes for 'metheglin', a mead extravaganza). Such bottles ferried claret and sack (a fortified Spanish white, like sherry) from the owner's cellar or from local wine merchants and taverns. In either instance, it became common for the owner of the bottle to fix a seal or button of glass to the bottle to ensure it returned to its rightful house (see pages 80–1). Both wines matured well in the cask, and anyway, there was no way to properly seal a bottle. Temporary stoppers, like oiled hemp, or wedges of cork, were tied to the rim of the neck, called the string course.

But when, in the late-seventeenth century, war with France and Spain made claret unpatriotic and highly taxed (just like brandy – see the Gin Craze pages 76–7), port (from Portugal) found its way to dominate the table. And port ages best when laid down in the bottle. This produced two innovations over the subsequent fifty years: a cork that would fit tightly in the bottle neck, and a bottle that would lie down properly to keep the cork moist. A standing bottle will dry the cork, letting in air and spoiling the wine. Bottles became cylindrical, mallet shaped, and the evolution of today's perfect form was begun.

WINE BOTTLE NECK

Around 1700

WINE BOTTLE SEAL

Around 1680

As mentioned on the previous page, wine bottle seals such as this were used to mark ownership of a bottle, not its contents. Wine was stored in casks, either in the cellar, if the owner had one big enough, or in a tavern. Bottles were carried and used to serve wine and were valuable in their own right. At table, a bottle with the owner's seal demonstrated status, much like an armorial dinner service. When you sent your servant to the tavern for a refill, you wanted to ensure he returned with your own bottle. Likewise, when a tavern served a bottle off premises, they wanted their bottle back, thank you very much. Hence seals. This seal is particularly literal, the R is probably the owner's surname. The I [J] and A, initials of (probably) husband and wife. It is far from clear if this is a private bottle or refers to tavern keepers: other seals were more explicit. Coats of arms were popular; symbols could refer to the sign of a tavern.

If the bottle on which this seal once sat proudly had belonged to a tavern, the owner would likely have been a member of the Vintners' Company. The company, one of 110 London livery companies (or guilds), was incorporated by Edward III to keep wine from being mixed and corrupted. Adulteration was common. The *Art and Mystery of Vintners and Wine-Coopers*, 1682, gives instructions for diluting wine to spread it more thinly: 'If you have three Butts of Malmosey you may make four if you please. . . . This way you may rid your Laggs and old Canary away' (it only took one butt to drown the Duke of Clarence). Buying from a member of the company gave confidence that you were getting the good stuff.

Joseph Addison, the tartest of essayists, expanded on the problem in an issue of *Tatler* in 1709:

> There is in this city a certain fraternity of chymical operators who work underground in holes, caverns, and dark retirements, to conceal their mysteries from the eyes and observation of mankind. These subterraneous philosophers are daily employed in the transmigration of liquors, and by the power of magical drugs and incantations, raise under the streets of London the choicest products of the hills and valleys of France. They can squeeze Bourdeaux out of a slow [sloe], and draw Champagne from an apple.

Hidden behind the crazing of this delftware piece is a beautiful chain of manganese purple links, spots of the same and vigorous brushstrokes of cobalt blue. It's a drug jar, which beyond fragments of dish and tile, is one of the most common sorts of delftware found on the foreshore. The jars, unbroken, devoid of craquelure, would have been the brightest advertisements in the windows and shelves of London's apothecary shops. They stood in ranks, with huge variation in size and pattern but just a few shapes, from the straight-sided dry jars like this to jars for syrups that looked like globes on stalks.

In their uniformity of shape and colour they achieved an early form of brand identity. Nurofen does the same today: their packets joining visually together across a chemist's shelf, each linked in a continuous wave of pain-targeting micro-missiles. And were the contents to the same purpose as Nurofen's, to seek and destroy a hangover? Some were, which is why I've included this jar here: all serious indulgers need a friend in the pharmacist.

The *Pharmacopoea Londinensis* was published around the time that this jar was made. It was the first 'official' list of appropriate medicines that members of the newly formed Worshipful Society of Apothecaries of London could dispense. The society was chartered in 1617, the *Pharmacopoea* published a year later. The famous herbalist and astrologer Nicholas Culpeper, writing from his house 'on the East side of Spittle-Fields, neer London' translated it from Latin into English in 1649 for the good of his countrymen's health (though he bemoans its cost to his own). Hangover cures came mainly from the brassica family: lettuce and cabbage, although tree ivy ('Your best way is to boyl them in the same liquor you got your surfet by drinking') will do the job, and amethyst, worn, keeps men from drunkenness and is 'profitable in huntings and fightings'.

What else might these jars have held? Every type of plant and herb imaginable, and the eyes widen at the animal parts: the horn of harts or unicorns (of course); the skull of a man who was never buried; vulture '(if you can catch 'em)' and so, so many types of turds, his word, not mine. Pass me the unbranded ibuprofen.

APOTHECARY JAR

Blue and manganese apothecary jar
Delftware
Mid-seventeenth century

RASPBERRY PRUNT

From a German or Dutch forest glass roemer
Late-sixteenth to early-seventeenth century

I once used a goblet with things like this attached to try to get contemporary art buyers interested in old European furniture. This is a raspberry prunt. Eight or ten of these would have been set onto the stem of a seventeenth-century wine glass, or roemer. They were beautiful ornaments, but they also helped the greasy-fingered wealthy keep hold of their wine glasses before the adoption of forks at the dinner table. It is without doubt my favourite-ever find. It is jewel-like without being as gaudy as a gem; it is tactile beyond belief. To rub a thumb across its dimples is like caressing rosary beads or *tasbih*. It is talismanic. If it's out of its cabinet I can't take my hands off it. Full of contradictions. Incredible that so fragile a piece of glass should survive four hundred years of tides without being worn to a dull pebble.

When I first saw complete roemers (often pronounced 'rummer', the name comes from the Dutch for making a toast, roemen) in the auction house where I was working, I knew their appeal went far beyond dedicated collectors. They reminded me of the Campana Brothers' chandeliers for Lord Rothschild at Waddesdon, great explosions of material. Fat bowls of greenish glass on thick stems, either lumped with sharp twists of glass that could be by H.R. Giger, or these dimpled raspberry prunts. Even saying 'raspberry prunt' aloud is a sensual delight, all pops and sibilants.

Delicate glass roemers were a sign of wealth. They were imported, made in Germany or the Low Countries. They're often seen in those quiet, contemplative still lifes of the Dutch golden age. They dot Vermeer's paintings. Roemers are very very old, and extraordinarily modern. I got a contemporary art specialist to email his clients about the ones I was trying to promote. Some sold, some didn't. Love is a fickle thing.

This small fan of brown ties into a culture from deep in our
Northern European history, even though it was made comparatively
recently (it probably dates from the seventeenth century). What you can
see is the beard (and bared teeth) from a Bartmann jug: a fat bellied
jar with a bearded man on the front. Bartmann is German for beard man –
the Wild Man or woodwose of mediæval mythology; jugs such as this
were imported on a grand scale and used for carrying beer and the like.

Wild Men were part human, but were possessed of unreasonable
strength and terrible sexual energy and were unable to control their animal
urges. There is no pre-Christian record of the Wild Man but he seems on a
continuum with the Green Man (turn the foliage into hair and the transition
is complete) and shares with him a vitality sucked directly out of nature.
Like the Green Man, Wild Men were a staple of church architecture. They
can still be seen on misericords, sometimes in battle with dragons, as if to
suggest that, however rough they were, at least their allegiances were correct.
Early Christian scholars associated Wild Men with Greco-Roman satyrs
and fauns in a manner that I think was an attempt to tie them to a classical
tradition rather than pagan. They were a bogeyman to frighten people back
to God: neglect your soul and suffer madness.

More than a misericord, a beer jug seems the natural place to find a
Wild Man. Drink deep and find your inner woodwose. In mediæval Europe,
beyond madness, only drunkenness gave you the licence to act without
reason, to obey urges, to disgrace yourself and be forgiven. Unless, of course,
you pushed the amnesia of societal forgiveness too far and found yourself
expelled, ostracised, forced to wander the woods like a real Wild Man.

The jugs were made in the Rhineland, where the legend of the Wild Man
was very strong. Some suggest they were marked with his face as a symbol
of the *genius loci* – the spirit of the place. Certainly Bartmann jugs were so
important to Frechen, the town where they were made the longest, that its
coat of arms is a lion holding a Bartmann jug.

The mythology doesn't end there. Emptied of their contents, Bartmann
jugs were used as witch bottles, filled with gruesome contents: urine, nail
clippings, pins, and buried in the walls and floors of houses for protection.

BARTMANN JUG BEARD

Stoneware, probably Frechen, Germany
Seventeenth century

TEAPOT

Jackfieldware glazed earthenware teapot
Jackfield Pottery, Staffordshire
1750–60

I particularly like how this piece balances. It is entirely fragmentary, and yet this single leg and fat underbelly of a Jackfield teapot manages to conjure up a ghostly impression of the whole. Jackfield pots are an unusual branch of the slipware family. Rather than exhibiting the thrilling contrasting colours of poured or combed slipware, it is a ruddy earthenware clay entirely covered in luscious glossy black slip. It has the glowing unctuousness of an advertisement for Magnum.

In the mid-eighteenth century, when this pot was fired, tea drinking in England was already a hundred years old. The (hot) water of life had arrived around the same time as those other two hot drinks, coffee and chocolate. All three were bitter, so all required sugar. The growth of consumption therefore mirrored the growth in sugar imports, and so the growth in slavery. But where coffee was an affordable stimulant in the capital's coffee houses, tea was horrendously expensive, and restricted at first to the locked tea caddies of the aristocracy. With women's movements restricted by a deeply conservative society (for all the perceived gaiety of the eighteenth century), women met primarily in the home and tea became the centrepiece of their gatherings. The ritual of drinking tea echoed the ceremonies of China. It was taken in imported porcelain or elegant domestic inspirations, like this Jackfield pot.

At the same time, tea was undergoing economic convulsions. Taxes added 100 per cent to the cost and contraband was rife. Vast swathes of the country were effectively turned into a police state by excise officers whose investigations dragged through the countryside like a red-hot rake. Smugglers were killed in mass executions. By the 1780s taxes had been reduced and tea-running was eliminated, but the result of this was that spending on tea went up. As all tea came from China, and the Chinese demanded payment in silver bullion, this increase in tea drinking was a grave threat to the exchequer's reserves. The solution was opium. Grown and manufactured by the British in India, a flood of opium was exported to the Chinese (with payment in silver, please). Trade was balanced, and when the Chinese eventually kicked, the Opium Wars guaranteed both commerce and the eventual downfall of a millennia-old civilisation.

Lid with grapes and vines
Nineteenth century

Much of the perverse pleasure of mudlarking is found in the desire for objects to be things they inexplicably are not. It is very difficult to identify things from fragments, even the experts I talk to sometimes struggle. I really want this to be the top of a snuff box and for a long time identified it as such. But it cannot be, it was made one hundred years too late. Snuff began as a late-seventeenth-century fashion. The aristocracy shifted from smoking tobacco in a pipe to taking it as snuff from elegant little boxes, mainly precious metal, some pottery. I find so many pipes that I long for a more upmarket tobacco accessory. Not this one, I'm afraid.

Snuff is a powdered, spiced tobacco, sniffed by the pinch. The perfumes in it were incredible, from sinus-clearing cumin and mustard to bergamot, orange blossom and jasmine. Like the pipe, it was first promoted as medicinal before becoming ubiquitous. What's interesting is that although the fashion spread down the class ladder, as fashions are wont to do, there remained a town and country divide with snuff. Countrymen, even the well off, continued to smoke pipes – indeed were renowned and looked down on for it. But the cliques of London had discovered the joys of the short, sharp sniff. Like today's favourite nasal powder, snuff was both a cherished social lubricant and profoundly unethical.

Where contemporary Londoners delight in the unexamined snorting of cocaine produced by Mexico's Zetas (the ex-special forces drug cartel that has killed tens of thousands in gory spectaculars), eighteenth-century snuff-takers were the beneficiaries of systemic slavery. In British colonies across the West Indies and America close to half a million Africans were enslaved in plantations of tobacco, sugar and other goods newly essential for the European home. Vast wealth was accumulated by plantation owners, speculators, merchants and bankers. Most of which survives today in forms both concrete and cultural: the country houses, the patronage-assisted scientific advances, the leisure-fed age of enlightenment.

Georgian England is seen so much as a Golden Age. In almost any sphere of art or culture, the classical taste of the eighteenth century could be claimed as a pinnacle. It is difficult, I think, for one to be sensitive to the intelligence of Georgian architecture, the wit of Georgian gardens, and hold the thought of how rotten are their foundations. There's an awful sense of edifice-pulling. Because it's undeniable: no fashions were higher, no sensibilities more refined. And yet. There's putrefaction under there. Perhaps the snuff helped take away the smell of it.

CLAY TOBACCO PIPES

Mudlarking is above all a cumulative experience.
My earliest hauls from the beaches were clay pipe stems.
Hundreds of them. They're easy to spot and easy to
distinguish (being long white tubes) against the buff-
and-amber-coloured gravel. If you put this book down
and take a Tube to near the South Bank and hop over
the wall (assuming when you get there that the tide is
out), you'll come back with pipe stems too. And they're
entrancing, because before you picked one up it had been
held by no one except the Londoner who dropped it in
the river two hundred years ago. Just your hands, and his
hands, and nothing in between. Can you feel that?

I felt it. That's why I kept being drawn back to the river, even after finding nothing but pipe stems. But gradually, I got better at spotting objects that weren't gravel, and weren't pipe stems. Pottery, first of all. So much pottery is in the river! And then came the compulsion to find pipe bowls, because stems are fine, but they become a little repetitive. But a bowl! That's a real find.

And finding it is a hunger. And I've seen that hunger grow in so many new mudlarks, to have an object that is not just old and connected to an individual, but that has an aesthetic quality, a functional quality of its own. You're not going to use the stems as straws for a milkshake, but you could smoke from a pipe bowl.

I've heard a lot about people giving them a try, when they've finally found one, and after it has been thoroughly cleaned (because would smouldering in the bowl sterilise everything the Thames has to offer? I think it's doubtful). Standing with the smokers outside an art gallery in Mayfair a man told me he'd once found a pile of well-used bowls at the base of some steps on the north shore. Later, on a pleasant evening with a low tide, he'd discovered why: around the steps convened a meeting of comrades to smoke crack and enjoy the weather.

An incredible image. It makes you think of the debauchery, the sheer baby-over-the-banisters intoxication of Hogarth's *Gin Lane*. This is the true London. The London that everybody searches for

'My favourite is his servant's first discovery of Raleigh at study with his pipe. Horrified by the sight of smoke, the servant jumped to the conclusion that his master was on fire and doused him with a tankard of ale.'

when they embark on psychogeographical explorations or algorithmical walks. When people put on their black hooded tops and GoPros for a spot of urban exploration in tunnels or up the drainpipe of a condemned building, they're not just doing it for the thrill of the trespass, they're doing it because they know that there's another London there. That if they can just find a route across time's semi-permeable membrane they can walk alongside Hawksmoor as he plots his mysteries (it's no coincidence that the Masters of the Universe's deals continue to be sealed over rib-eye steak at Hawksmoor Spitalfields). Maybe they'll be able to sit at Ashmole's Invisible College.

But there isn't a pipe to be seen in *Gin Lane*. Tobacco was too wholesome. Instead a pipe takes pride of place clamped between John Bull the blacksmith's teeth in *Gin Lane's* sister print, the less well-known *Beer Street*. This is Hogarth's vision of true Britishness. The very architecture confounds today's occultish romantics: the subtlety of St Martin-in-the-Fields takes the backdrop to *Beer Street* in contrast to Hawksmoor's decadent St George's Bloomsbury in *Gin Lane*.

And dominating *Beer Street* is our man of enormous appetites, his apron strained tight against his belly, sleeves rolled up over a hard-won bicep. He reclines under a pub sign, Health to the Barley Mow ('Here's health to the barley mow, my boys . . . We'll drink it out of the jolly brown bowl' goes the drinking song), in one hand a pewter tankard of beer so large and foamy it looks like a cooling tower, in the other a vast leg of mutton. And in his mouth, defiantly, priapically, a long clay pipe is raised to the skies.

It wasn't always like this.

Tobacco was first introduced to England during the reign of Queen Elizabeth I. Tobacco made it over from the New World thanks to Christopher Columbus, and began seriously to spread in the second half of the sixteenth century. Like so many introductions (mineral water, chocolate), it launched with a narrative about health benefits, became fashionable, and finally settled as an everyman's necessity. Perhaps because it was seen as a cure, a smoker was said to drink tobacco (albeit alight, and from a pipe).

Sir Francis Drake and Sir Walter Raleigh are often credited with introducing tobacco to this country, but it seems more likely that we simply adopted a growing European fashion. Even if not the originator, Raleigh certainly secured tobacco's success at court, to the extent of making a convert of Elizabeth herself. Apocryphal stories attach themselves to him; my favourite is his servant's first discovery of Raleigh at study with his pipe. Horrified by the sight of smoke, the servant jumped to the conclusion that his master was on fire and doused him with a tankard of ale. He certainly drank that pipe.

The first pipes used in England were in some way mimics of Native American pipes – and actual Native American pipes of the period have been found here. Within ten years pipe makers and their customers had settled on a design that would remain essentially standard until today: a little fat-bellied barrel. Something that could hold a plug of tobacco and burn it evenly. You could look at the briar pipe your grandfather smoked and recognise the barrel-bowled pipe as its venerable relation. At first these pipes were minuscule because tobacco was so expensive and its purpose medicinal. Drink a 'whiffe' of smoke and feel the purge. Their bowl-holes were just over half a centimetre; they've been known as fairie pipes.

Smoking was not without controversy. The Elizabethan playwright Ben Jonson, he of the Canary-wine, put forth the pros and cons in his 1598 play *Every Man in his Humour*. Captain Bobadill, the boastful coward, introduces the art of smoking. Beyond saying that while in the Indies he ate nothing but Trinidado smoke for twenty-one weeks, and that it will make an antidote to 'the most deadly poisonous plant in all Italy', he affirms it 'to be the most sovereign and precious weed that ever the earth tendered to the use of man'.

But enter Cash and Cob. Cob, the low clown of the play, says of Bobadill's pipe: 'It's good for nothing but to choke a man and fill him full of smoke and embers – there were four died out of one house, last week, with taking of it . . . he voided a bushel of soot yesterday, upward and downward.'

James 1, Elizabeth's successor, took Cob's side. He banned smoking in ale-houses and in 1604 printed a 'counterblaste' for his Court, where he described it as: 'A custom loathsome to the eye, hateful to the nose, harmful to the brain, dangerous to the lungs, and in the black, stinking fume thereof, nearest resembling the horrible Stygian smoke of the pit that is bottomless.'

But just as today, whatever the Crown's feelings about the pernicious weed, it had to hold its nose when it came to outright outlawing.

In his distaste, James I increased the rate of tax from 2d per pound to 6s 8d. According to Sandra Bell in her article *The Subject of Smoke*, the Venetian ambassador to England in 1618 reported that tobacco duty yielded the King 40,000 golden crowns a year. Tobacco was being sold, exclusively, in 7,000 houses in and around London, as well as in every 'Taverne, Inne, and Alehouse . . . Apothecaries Shops, Grosers Shopes, Chaundlers Shops'.

A tobacco box became an important part of a fashionable man's outfit. They were in use soon after the introduction of tobacco and sought after by all who drank the stuff, conveniently holding their stash. In the ale-houses, boxes holding a pound of tobacco and a selection of new pipes sat on tables for customers' pleasure: drop a penny in to unlock the lid and help yourself to the drawer of tobacco. Customers took just enough for a single smoke; as with newspaper racks in the US, unsupervised honesty was expected.

For all his dislike of smoking, James I granted a Royal Charter to the Tobacco-pipe Makers of Westminster in the County of Middlesex, thereby damping the careers of the pipe makers elsewhere. Charles I maintained this London monopoly and saw the pipe makers become a City of London Company. The Chartered Company had the right to break and enter places where they suspected illegal pipes were being made, but they were fighting a losing battle. By the mid-seventeenth

'It's good for nothing but to choke a man and fill him full of smoke and embers – there were four died out of one house, last week, with taking of it . . .'

century there were over a thousand pipe makers in London, and many more around the country. Like many potters of the day, pipe makers were itinerant. They moved where they could find the clay and the custom.

Because ceramic technology was so limited, the design of pipes didn't really change for a hundred years. And then came the Restoration and two things happened. First, snuff, a continental delicacy, became the fashionable way to feed the addiction. Just as with wigs (see pages 202–3), when Charles II returned he brought with him the highest of French fashions to poor repressed England. Snuff was French, and pipe smoking quickly fell from grace in London, suitable only as comfort for the working man at toil or salve for the merchant.

The second big change was the evolving design of the pipe. The belly slimmed, the bowl lengthened, and around the turn of the eighteenth century, the bowl went from leaning eagerly forwards to sitting upright. Clay manufacturing had improved and pipes could become long, thin and delicate. They were ready for a century of Georgian elegance. This is the pipe of *Beer Street*.

Early pipes had had a beautiful little milled rim to their bowls (see page 100), but it wasn't until the mid-eighteenth century that they began to develop a personality. First maker's marks became

'By the nineteenth century pipes had become objects of extraordinary artistry, collectors' items of the day, signs of association, allegiance, favour and style.'

common, on the heel of the pipe, and then came full-body decoration. By the nineteenth century pipes had become objects of extraordinary artistry, collectors' items of the day, signs of association, allegiance, favour and style. From a trail of elegant oak-leaves at the front of the bowl, or classical fluting around it, to faces, hooves, claws, scales and historical events. The Royal Antediluvian Order of Buffaloes (page 104) – think Freemasons but set up by a couple of comedy actors – had pipes made solely for ceremonial use: to be kissed as 'to what you will ultimately return, namely, Clay', and to be broken, wrapped in a ribbon.

The first pipes were expensive and social; they were passed around and shared. By the time the age of clay came to an end, they had become a free commodity. Pubs could give away ten thousand a year to their customers. By the end of the nineteenth century, pipe smoking had returned to the intelligentsia. Briar took off in the 1880s, Meerschaum came over from Europe. Sherlock Holmes kept the pipe alight until James I's dire predications paid off and tobacco's true benefits became apparent. We've been left with a chronology of bowls, and beaches of stems for everyone to get that first touch of history.

CLAY TOBACCO PIPES

1610–40

I love this detail of the overlapping milling.

1700–70

Pipe makers begin to tease elegance from their clay.

1780–1820

The first complete pipe I found.

1820–40

John Ford of Stepney, one of London's biggest pipe-making brands.

CLAY TOBACCO PIPES

1840–80

I just love these oak leaves and acorns.
They're so English.

After 1840

This gadrooning is just exquisite.

CLAY TOBACCO PIPES

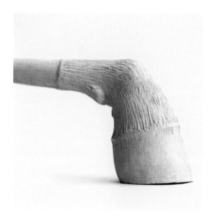

After 1840

The horse's hoof. Where it all started for me.

After 1840

The Royal Antediluvian Order of Buffaloes, made to be ceremonially broken.

1850–1910

The foliage holds the bowl with an incredible delicacy.

1850–1910

Extremely sparse decoration, with almost invisible 'eyelets'.

PLEASURES OF THE TABLE

As I write, I have the option, according to TripAdvisor, of visiting any one of 18,182 restaurants in London. I'm not sure how religiously I would follow their recommendations, but if their statistics are a good approximation to reality then there is one place to eat for every 469 Londoners. We are well supplied. Restaurants range from Rules, London's oldest, founded in 1798, to Ariana II, on the Kilburn High Road, probably the best Afghan restaurant in town. Rules started life as an oyster restaurant, when oysters were brought up to Billingsgate Market by the million (see pages 114–15). It's now renowned for (besides unctuous comfort) its extremely fine game. How English. Yet only a decade after Thomas Rule set oysters upon his bar, a Bengal restauranteur opened London's first curry house, the Hindoostane Coffee House. London has always been astonishingly open to new cultures and their cuisines.

London's gastronomic renown began with exports. Roman traders took Kentish oysters and Thames salt and sent them around the Empire. The advantage to being established as a trading hub is that it positively encourages an osmotic exchange of cultures, resulting in a substantial layer of Romanised Britons. All of whom were eager consumers of Roman luxuries like wine, oil and olives.

In the first and second centuries, substantial docks and warehouses were built on the Thames near London Bridge to manage goods both in and out. Germany provided wine in barrels made of silver fir and millstones for grinding flour. Spain sent *garum*, a fish sauce, fermented, rich in natural MSG. It was made by salting the intestines of the fish and leaving them to fester for months in the hot Mediterranean sunshine. Fish sauce returned to London with the rise in Southeast Asian restaurants; the Kingsland Road gives ample opportunity to enjoy the salty umami hit. Tablewares were also imported, scarlet Samian wares from Gaul (another staple of the modern Thames that I've yet to find) and bronze, glass and other potteries from the rest of the Empire.

The Romans also brought ideas with them: how we might produce staples locally and remove the need for imports. The bottom of the flagon (see pages 42–3) is an example of this, probably made in England for wine grown in English vineyards. When the Roman Empire collapsed, many of the technologies they had brought were lost. London had a black

'London had a black period – literally, a couple of hundred years in the strata where little is seen on the site of the Roman city but black soil, rotted vegetation.'

period – literally, a couple of hundred years in the strata where little is seen on the site of the Roman city but black soil, rotted vegetation. Saxon communities were dotted around the suburbs however. Centred around Covent Garden, London, Lundenwic, became the chief city of the East Saxons by the seventh century. In the 730s, the Venerable Bede described Lundenwic as a 'mart of many nations'. It was the port of the Kingdom of Mercia, trading with other English nations as well as Frankish and Low Country markets. Commerce and good eating lasted until the Vikings came along, repeatedly plundering London in the ninth century, returning again in the eleventh to give us Cnut, King of England (London held out for a bit) and most of Scandinavia.

On Bede's death in Jarrow in AD 735, he gave the community of monks there his most precious possession: his box of peppercorns. This was an extraordinarily rare and expensive spice in the eighth century. Pepper was a wild plant, growing in the rainforests of Malabar on the west coast of India; when Bede wrote of Lundenwic as a mart of many nations, it was no idle boast. But Londoners did not trade directly with India. London traded with other, nearby, markets, each one a node in a great ecosystem of trade that took in local goods and exchanged them for high-value imports. In this way, precious peppercorns could travel stop by stop until eventually finding their way to London. Pepper was probably acquired in Pavia, in Lombardy, from whence it would have come from Basra, Iraq, and before that, by boat from Kerala on the Malabar coast. Kerala is still known as the Spice Garden of India.

In the fifteenth century, Portuguese explorers opened up direct trade with Kerala. This was not just an expansionist move by the first European colonisers, it was also because of the collapse of the most famous trade route of all: the Silk Road. For 3,500 years, the Silk Road and its ancestors had been the route by which merchants carried goods between China and the Middle East. The last stretch into Europe terminated (typically) at Venice and Genoa, two sworn enemies. When the Byzantine and Mongol empires began to decline, the stability of the overground route wobbled, and then fell. The rush to replace it was in part responsible for Portugal's explosion of wealth, leading the way for the establishment of other European empires.

In William Harrison's *Description of England*, of 1587, he emphasises the self-sufficiency and plenty of the country, how since ancient times the Englishman has been fed on 'flesh and milk'. His lavish descriptions of a noble's meal give heartburn to the reader, but, at the close of the sixteenth century, also hint at the new bounties arriving from the Portuguese (Portingales, in Elizabethan terminology):

> In number of dishes and change of meat, the nobility of England
> (whose cooks are for the most part musical-headed Frenchmen
> and strangers) do most exceed, sith there is no day in manner
> that paseth over their heads wherein they have not only beef,
> mutton, veal, lamb, kid, pork, cony, capon, pig, or so many of these
> as the season yieldeth, but also some portion of the red or fallow
> deer, beside great variety of fish and wild fowl, and thereto sundry
> other delicates wherein the sweet hand of the seafaring Portingale
> is not wanting.

It was also *via* the Silk Road that Europeans first encountered Chinese porcelain. Unimaginably delicate, doubly so when compared to the heavy earthenwares of European potters, crisply coloured and sharply defined, porcelain was one of the most highly valued wares to come out of China. Just a trickle reached Europe until the Portuguese established their merchant reach; then trade grew rapidly. The commodity remained beyond all but the wealthiest, but it became a sign of great sophistication to use genuine china at the table. Responding to this market, the Chinese imperial potteries began producing porcelain especially for Europeans, which became known as 'exportware'. Europeans returned the favour by sending designs to China for manufacture, incorporating European taste and Chinese technology. Typically the designs were orientalist in the extreme, with Chinese painters decorating objects with a massively distorted view of Chinese daily life. China was extraordinarily closed off to outsiders, and I expect they thought Europeans must be very silly indeed if they believed that Chinese people lived the way they were depicted. The most famous orientalist picture of all, the omnipresent Willow Pattern, takes this up on pages 132–3.

The growth of European colonial powers didn't just change the dishes on which we ate, it also changed the dishes we consumed. In particular it brought the four great drinks: coffee, chocolate, tea and tobacco (it being common in the seventeenth century to take a 'drink' of tobacco smoke, see page 95), and the ruin of us all: sugar. Sweetener of diabetes, heart disease, obesity and tooth decay, born of rank plantations and slavery. Replacement of fat in 'light' comestibles (fruit yoghurt: five teaspoons of sugar; the low-fat version: six and a half teaspoons of sugar), foundation of Croesus-like wealth and benefactor of the arts, giver of galleries. Ah, sugar. The spun-sugar structures that supported the plantations, slavery and trade are discussed over a sugar cone mould on pages 122–3.

Tobacco has a chapter to itself (pages 92–105); tea is the focus of the Jackfield teapot in 'Pleasure and Vice' (pages 88–9): it was a private, domestic drink. Coffee and chocolate were for public consumption. Coffee was Arabic, chocolate from newly discovered South America. Coffee houses began opening in London in the 1660s. They followed the Middle Eastern model, typically signed by a Turk's head or a Turkish coffee pot, and like Arabic houses, they were places for conversation and debate as much as drinking. Coffee was cherished for inspiring great feats of wit, and coffee houses rapidly developed individual traditions, clientèles and political allegiances. These coffee houses were the direct progenitors of the gentlemen's club: all male enclaves with formidably distinctive characters. Alcohol consumption fell as men spent all day and long into the night entertaining their fellows over nothing more potent than coffee hot as hell and black as the devil. If the caffeine had them holding on to

'In particular it brought the four great drinks: coffee, chocolate, tea and tobacco ... and the ruin of us all: sugar. Sweetener of diabetes, heart disease, obesity and tooth decay, born of rank plantations and slavery.'

the walls for support, they could switch to chocolate. Chocolate came from the cacao bean, discovered by Europeans with the Spanish conquest of the Aztecs. Both chocolate and beans were used as currency by the Aztec elite – it was paid in tribute, or used to buy consumables, like a 'tolerable good slave' for 100 beans. The taste for chocolate spread from Spain (where it arrived about 1600) throughout Europe; like most things at that time, England turned up late. Taking chocolate started around 1650 in London. In coffee houses chocolate became a side-line, not the drink of purpose.

The seventeenth century also saw a substantial expansion of London (into the 'suburbs' close by the City and Westminster). Due to overcrowding, an increasing proportion of the population lived in lodging houses without communal kitchens. Lodgers could pay for 'board', but it was often stingy. For these Londoners, eating out wasn't a lifestyle choice, it was a necessity. Victualling-houses ranged from the most basic, where a customer might expect to get a porringer of broth but the knives were chained to the tables (see pages 130–1), to the cook shops with spits of meat of every type. There was no snobbery associated with cook shops, customers cut as much meat off the spit as they liked and ate it with a roll and a bottle of beer. According to the French traveller Henri Misson, even a 'Gentleman of 1500 Livres a Year enters a Cook's Shop without fear of being despis'd for it, and there dines for his Shilling to his Heart's Content'. Servants might congregate in a bun house on their mornings off,

'According to the French traveller Henri Misson, even a "Gentleman of 1500 Livres a Year enters a Cook's Shop without fear of being despis'd for it, and there dines for his Shilling to his Heart's Content".'

eager to display a new piece of finery over a 'Chelsey Bunn'. Street hawkers were to be found everywhere, selling oysters (pages 114–15), pies, or even fresh meat for customers to take into a tavern for roasting.

Reading Henry Mayhew's ninteenth-century *London Labour and the London Poor*, one encounters precisely the same sort of street sellers as stood outside taverns in the 1600s. No doubt they still cried the same cries. Time improved cook shops, however. When Misson wrote his guide, he thought there was only one restaurant in London where it was worth spending one or two guineas per head, the 'famous Pontac's'. Sixty years after the book was translated into English, Rule opened his oyster bar, and that's still going today. Eating was changing in London.

Now London is one of the few cities at the forefront of modern gastronomy. Many of the most interesting restaurants are in the suburbs of Westminster and Shoreditch; many still source their meat from Smithfield, their fish from Billingsgate (though the market has shifted east since oysters arrived there in their uncountable millions). Heston Blumenthal delights diners with his historical meals at Dinner (who hasn't seen a photograph of his meat tangerine, *circa* 1500?); elsewhere every country, including the ex-colonies and the ex-conquerers (the Scandinavian Kitchen on Great Titchfield Street gives you three adorable little open sandwiches for £5.95 at lunchtime), has its beachhead in a restaurant in London.

OYSTER SHELLS

Eighteenth to nineteenth century

The enormous consumption of oysters once seen in London is difficult to imagine today, when three of Colchester's finest will set you back nine pounds fifty at Wright Brothers. But during the Roman period, and again from the Middle Ages, oysters were eaten in vast, almost inconceivable quantities, by the rich, by the poor, and by everyone in between.

The history of the oyster is tied so closely to the history of this country that some Victorians even claimed it as the reason the Romans invaded Britain: it was *via* oysters from Rutupine (present-day Richborough in Kent) that the Romans were purported to have discovered this island. Having found it, they wanted control of our superior shellfish. But when the empire faded so did the appetite for oysters.

It grew again in the Middle Ages. As references to oysters creep into literature in the seventeenth century, we see a populace enamoured of them. Pepys famously ate oysters by the barrel (although they were quite *small* barrels). Oyster Day was celebrated every year on 5 August, St James's Day. It was the opening of the oyster season and the first day that oysters could be brought up river to Billingsgate Market and sold to delirious Londoners. A couple of people were expected to die in the crush each year.

The appetite for oysters grew even more rapidly from the middle of nineteenth century. The discovery of vast new beds between Shoreham and Havre caused a tremendous free-for-all, and the new railway between Brighton and London meant oysters could be taken straight up to town without the swingeing percentages levied by Billingsgate. The two combined caused massive market disruption. Mayhew quoted the total sold by costermongers as 124 million a year – at four for a penny, and never the finest ones, the ones of a 'good middling quality' – and everyone from prostitutes to impoverished vicars stopping off to gulp them down for breakfast, lunch and supper. Green oysters, which got their colour from a long rest in shallow sun-heated salt marshes, were for some reason a particular delicacy. At its peak, the oyster industry employed 120,000 people.

But with that peak came the beginnings of the collapse. Overfishing imperilled many beds; there were jolts in the nineteenth century, and then within a couple of years around 1920 an epidemic of disease destroyed the south coast oyster beds. Although they have been nursed back to life, the four-a-penny oyster doesn't look to be returning soon.

Pottery was slow to develop real artistry in England. Until the sixteenth century, and the arrival of potters from Antwerp and the first delftware, most pottery was made by itinerant craftsmen who followed raw materials and the market. They would set up in places where they could dig good clay and fire utilitarian earthenwares. Some, like the porringer on pages 130–1, are rather fine and delicate in quality, but many were rough, made with clay that had as many inclusions as Rocky Road ice cream.

So, when spurred on by Dutch innovations, potters began to experiment with higher quality ceramics, there wasn't a pottery tradition to look back on. Instead, they looked to fashionable silversmiths for their inspiration. These craftsmen were often French, whose exclusive and ornate styles found favour with the elite. Their creations changed the way the English ate. Table settings became lavishly tiered with silver dish rings, sauce boats, cruets and great centrepieces added to the table. Forks, of all things, weren't accepted in England until post-Reformation French fashion brought them into vogue. In a stroke, they ended messy fingers at table and made wine glass prunts redundant (pages 84–5). Imagine trying to drink from a gripless glass with hands slathered in mutton fat.

Then there were standing salts. These had had a place on the English table since mediæval times; guests dipped their fingers in for a pinch of salt. The earliest type were the great salts, single, towering ornaments that stood by the host at high table. Favoured guests sat above the salt; less so, below. Hence the phrase. Eventually great salts gave way to trencher salts, one placed between every two guests. A style that bridged both was the scroll salt: a raised bowl with three or four arms rising from the rim, each scrolling outwards at the tip. They too were French; it's thought that Queen Henrietta Maria introduced them to Charles I.

Some of the most famous silver scroll salts were made in the 1630s, the same period that delftware scroll salts were being made. Like their silver cousins, they had three scrolled arms rising from the rim of an hourglass-shaped bowl. You can see one spiralling scroll in the photograph opposite. I think it's possible to imagine the merchant's brief to the potter: 'Make me,' he would have said, pointing to a silver scroll salt, 'make me one of these'.

SCROLL FROM A SCROLL SALT

Delftware
Mid-seventeenth century

PIPKIN HANDLE

Lead-glazed pipkin handle
Sixteenth to eighteenth century

What you see here is the handle of the Tudor slow cooker, the pipkin. I find everything about this object appealing. The adorably diminutive name pops suggestively from the lips with two explosive plosives. And just look at it. Imagine this little fellow standing proud on a fat-bellied kettle. To me it is a single earthenware entendre. An obvious goading of the less-well endowed.

And yet, according to Eric Partridge's *Dictionary of Slang and Unconventional English*, this is a complete misreading of the pipkin's sexual symbolism. The Tudors saw low humour in this lowly pot – but for reasons best known to themselves joked about a *woman's* pipkin, not a man's. The past truly is a foreign country.

When not appropriated to the vernacular, the pipkin was a common pot used much like a casserole. It had three stubby legs to support it and just a single handle. Pipkins were typically shuffled into the coals so as to cook at a gentle heat. They were extremely versatile, used for everything from sweets to savoury to spiced wines. Gervase Markham's *The English Housewife* of 1615 has wonderful cooking suggestions for the pipkin, including apple tarts ('take of the fairest Damask Prunes you can get, and put them in a clean pipkin, with fair water'); broth ('take a quart of fat kid broth'); 'smored' mallard ('put it into a pipkin with the neck downward'); lamb's head and 'an excellent boiled salad'.

The pots were glazed by dusting them with powdered lead oxide, usually only on the inside. This one is rather fine and beautifully yellow. The pottery is thinner and more delicate than usual. Adding copper filings to the glaze produced the rich, gorgeous green so distinctive to Tudor greenware.

In the mid-1500s, a good century before England established trade with China, Portuguese merchants had bases on the Chinese coast. Dealing with China was extremely desirable, vastly wealth-making and inexpressibly difficult. Foreigners had access only to confined 'factories', primarily in Canton; even in factories trade had to be through licensed Hongs, no other Chinese could deal with foreign merchants. The East India Company secured a trading post in Taiwan in 1672, moved to Canton around 1700, and held a monopoly on English trade for 160 years.

From the first Portuguese voyages, European elites developed a taste for exotic Chinese wares, particularly porcelain. The material was a revelation: translucently thin yet surprisingly tough, waterproof, heatproof, finely decorated. Compared to the earthenwares being made in Europe it was like a miracle. Scientists and entrepreneurs spent hundreds of years trying to replicate it, and while they tried, genuine china was being bought up as fast as it could be imported. It was shipped in the same vessels that carried tea. Unlike the precious leaf, porcelain was considered ballast, stored at the lowest point of the hold, impervious to leakage. Porcelain was perhaps a sideshow to the silver, opium and tea trade (pages 88–9), but to make a truly great profit one had to be master of all, connoisseur, gourmet and drug dealer.

Blue-and-white pottery was the prime porcelain import until the beginning of the eighteenth century; as trade became more established, designs began to be commissioned by European vendors. Polychrome porcelain began to take off with the rise of outsourced armorial pottery: families would send to China for dinner services decorated with their coats of arms. From this came a growth of vibrant coloured enamels, the *familles vert*, *rose* and the like, all perhaps linked to Western tastes in interior decorations. In reverse, a century later, English potteries would produce ceramics designed for local Asian markets, patterns assiduously researched and replicated.

Communication was always difficult, guarantees of quality and specification difficult to achieve, but for those who were successful in establishing trusted relationships, profits could be enormous. There are similarities with commissioning China's manufacturing capacity today. The hopeful startup places its order through Alibaba, where anything can be sourced, but it keeps its fingers tightly crossed until delivery comes through.

CHINESE EXPORT PORCELAIN

Late Ming Dynasty, seventeenth or eighteenth
century

SUGAR CONE MOULD

Made in Woolwich and Deptford
Seventeenth to nineteenth century

This fragment, to my eye, is one of the most exquisite in my collection. The delicate white brushstrokes appear as if a detail of Titian's drapery, or an abstract by Franz Kline. The juicy reds and thick black core (produced by 'reduction' firing, that is, firing without oxygen) can only be seen because the piece is broken; it reveals more in fragment than complete. Yet for all its beauty, this object carries associations with one of England's worst excesses: the sugar trade. It comes from a sugar cone mould: sugar cones stood in the neck of large jars at Thames-side sugar refineries; molasses would drip through a hole into the jar, leaving a hard cone of sugar behind.

In sugar, as in so many things, England followed where Spain and Portugal led. In the fifteenth century, they had set up sugar cane farms in Madeira and the Canary Islands; from thence Christopher Columbus took cane seedlings to the West Indian island of Hispaniola (now Haiti and the Dominican Republic). In the sixteenth century, Portugal put Brazil to the cane. A hundred years later, the Dutch attacked and seized the assets; looking to expand further they worked with the young Englishman James Drax to plant up the English colony, Barbados. On the back of these plantations, Drax would become one of the wealthiest men in England.

Barbados established a model that other Caribbean islands followed. English entrepreneurs sailed out to the West Indies with indentured servants, and on the profits of their servants' labour would invest in slaves, and on the profits of their slave labour would expand their plantations and see themselves and their families rich for generations.

Slaves were chattel, to be bought and sold, subjugated, beaten, worked to death. In his book *The Sugar Barons*, Matthew Parker quotes a slave as saying: 'The Devel was in the English-man, that he makes every thing work; he makes the Negro work, the Horse work, the Ass work, the Wood work, the Water work, and the Winde work.' Slavers traded men, women and children from Africa to West Indian planters; packed onto boats, shackled in their own filth, the slave ship was the hell-mouth through which few free-born Africans returned. If they survived the journey, they entered a Boschian hell of blood and burning: hands sliced to the bone on sugar canes, limbs scalded to amputation by boiling sugar. Back in England, dainty sugar creations were admired at every table and wealth was accrued.

Sometimes what I love most about mudlarking is not finding the unique and historical and rare, it's being able to take something small and to get right to the bottom of it.

A lot of what is found on the beaches is super-hard to identify. But when there's writing, even the first-time mudlarker has the opportunity to put on Sherlock Holmes' deerstalker (metaphorically) and do some genuine detective work. Google a bit of writing, and it can turn a few square centimetres of glass into a three-act play complete with programme and cast notes. That's why I chose this piece. The other reason is that I love pickle.

If you squint, the glass reads 'nwaring /eckham'. That's enough to go on. First, guess the complete words and go fishing with them. Manwaring Peckham. It's something extraordinary. Listing after listing of auctions of complete bottles (who wants a complete bottle? Not me, not unless I've found it), but they're enough to confirm that you've got the name right. Then a souvenir brochure for the 1911 Festival of Empire has Manwaring's stall listing (Stall 109) and tells you that they made three products: ROYAL NAVAL PICKLE, NAVAL CHUTNEY and GORDON SAUCE – gosh, I bet they'd clear your sinuses. You also find out they were a contractor to the Admiralty, and established in 1864.

Keep looking, there's a promotional Manwaring's matchbox for sale. It has their address, so now we know they were on Sumner Road, Peckham. An archaeological report has them in trade directories in 1878 and 1908. Google Books tells you they moved a few roads over in 1932, to Radnor House, Hill Street, when a new factory was built for them (it was of the three-storey 'Daylight' type). And it gives clues enough take you to the Haywards Pickle site: in 1956 Manwaring and Haywards merged (the latter was a Kennington brand. Keeping it South London). Then sixty years of journeying through ownership: Brook Bond Oxo, Unilever. Now Mizkan Euro (sushi seasoning . . . and Branston).

And all this, from a piece of glass no longer than my thumb.

After 1864

William George Weedon & Co.
1890–1910

Roman London supplied its citizens with clean water. In the Dark Ages the town took water from wells and rivers: the Thames of course, and the Fleet, Walbrook, Langbourn and Oldbourne. By the thirteenth century those waters had become unsafe to drink. Lead pipes were constructed to bring water from Tyburn (present day Marble Arch) to the City. In the seventeenth century, the New River was constructed to bring water from Hertfordshire into the houses of the wealthy.

Romans also liked mineral water, but that delicacy was later in returning to England. Elizabeth I had it sent to Court from Buxton and in the mid-seventeenth century it became fashionable to 'take the waters' at spas. First at Bath, then at towns like Tunbridge Wells, Hampstead and Wanstead. Spa waters became the seltzer to Georgians' appetites. George Cheyne, in his *Essay of Health and Long Life* of 1724, advised drinking Bath-Water (no, not bathwater) as the only remedy for men 'forced to drink much Punch' which gave them 'Mortal dry-Belly-aches, Palsies, Cramps, and Convulsions'. Cheyne asserted that 'Water was the primitive, original Beverage, as it is the only Simple Fluid' though he astutely notes that although there are 'three more in nature, Mercury, Light, and Air, none is fit for human Drink'.

As mineral waters became mass-produced (see the torpedo bottle on pages 128–9) they evolved. Soon soft drinks like ginger beer, lemonade and sarsaparilla were sold around London. According to *Liquid Pleasures* by John Burnett, London had fifty producers in the 1840s employing 541 people. By 1890 almost 7,000 Londoners were employed making bottled minerals. This bottle dates from around then. And, oh what a beauty! Complete, sealed, and with all its original contents. Screw-stoppers were invented by Henry Barrett in the 1870s, and he patented the design in 1881. They're made of moulded vulcanite (or xylonite, or celluloid – Barrett didn't seem fussy) with a pink indiarubber washer. The indiarubber on my bottle is a fine Thames-mud black. So was the rest of the bottle – this mud, if you've never encountered it, is a thing to behold. Heavier than lead, stickier than glue and stains like the devil. Still, amazing stuff for preserving a couple of thousand years of history, so who's complaining?

In 1910, William George Weedon, a mineral water manufacturer from Stepney, went bankrupt. But before then, this bottle was filled, capped, and dropped into the Thames.

These bottles are a fantastic example of behavioural economics in design, not so much a nudge as a very Swiss 'if customers can't be trusted to do it right, force rightness onto them'. In a corrective to Orson Welles' Harry Lime, these bottles (and their artificially sparkling contents) were a Swiss invention, so you can add fizzy water to the cuckoo clock that five hundred years of democracy and peace has produced.

Fizzy water is natural, in some places. San Pellegrino has been producing naturally carbonated water for six centuries. But with a growing interest in the health benefits of mineral water in the eighteenth century, attempts were made to mechanise the production of sparkle. Joseph Priestley, most famous as the discoverer of oxygen (or phlogiston as he termed it), also invented a way of creating soda water, which he hoped would ward off scurvy on long voyages.

But Priestley's discoveries, published in 1772, took the interest of Jacob Schweppe, who was working as a watchmaker in Geneva. He simplified the requirements, industrialised them and founded his Schweppes company in 1783. Less than ten years later, the successful Schweppes moved to England, setting up at 141 Drury Lane.

He produced three strengths of soda water, and other drinks like seltzer, Spa and Rochelle Salt. Bottles were tightly sealed with a wired cork, like champagne today, but there was still a risk that all the gas would leak out by the time the bottle was opened. Schweppe did not want to give his customers a flat experience, so his solution was what became known as the drunken bottle: a bottle that just couldn't stand up.

The curved base of this bottle allows for thinner (and so more parsimonious) glass to be used while still being strong enough to hold pressurised gases. But more importantly, it ensured customers stored bottles on their sides, which meant the corks kept wet and perfectly sealed. All the lovely fizz stayed right where it belonged.

These bottles were also known as 'torpedo', 'egg-shaped' and 'Hamilton', the latter because a William F. Hamilton patented the design in 1809, even though their invention by Schweppe predated the patent. The use of Hamilton is dying slowly, perhaps because it seems somehow unfair that a man with only a bottle to his name should have it stripped away in favour of one whose name is still plastered on the front of every mixer in the supermarket.

TORPEDO BOTTLE BOTTOM

Nineteenth century

PORRINGER

Lead-glazed
Mid-sixteenth to eighteenth century

O What's the rhyme to porringer?
Ken ye the rhyme to porringer?
King James the Seventh had ae dochter,
And he gave her to an Oranger.

Jacobite song

The song mourns the loss of a Catholic dream. James ii (James vii of Scotland) fled and in came Protestant William and Mary: William of Orange and Mary the dochter. It also has an absolutely ingenious rhyme for the famously unrhymable orange.

Porringer sounds deliciously close to porridge and is often associated with it: a shallow bowl with a single handle holding the wateriest of mush for the lowest of classes. Think of the bowl held out by Oliver Twist, a porringer of thin gruel and please some more. Porringers seem particularly resonant today, with the number of food banks having grown from 29 in 2008 – the year the collapse of the market for Collateralised Debt Obligations caused a massive diversion of funds from the public to the banks – to 445 in 2015, handing out a million emergency food packages. They're resonant too in the way we look at relative poverty across the world: at nations where primary meals are still boiled grain and water (Dal, Congee, Nshima) and ones where we've forgotten such want ever existed. Can you really look at London and see people dying of starvation less than two hundred years ago? People's memories are short.

For a penny and a half in the eighteenth century you could have a porringer full of meat and broth at a cellar known as Porridge Island. Edmund Burke recommended a half penny porringer of pease-soup and potatoes, and 'praise the wholesomeness of your frugal repast'. But they weren't all frugal. King Charles ii ate 'spoon meat' from his porringer. The Lady Compton insisted upon them for her Lemon Cream. The difference was in material. Poor people used earthenware, the wealthy, pewter.

Earthenware porringers had all sorts of recorded uses, for grinding gunpowder, for collecting blood when it was let. Francis Bacon even used one to set two flames within each other to show that 'flame doth not mingle with flame'. Porringers did not mingle either: pease-soup in one, lemon cream in another. Today, London is home to food banks and Fortnum's.

For a time, I imagine, it would have been impossible to pass a day in Britain, as one of the middle classes, without encountering the Willow Pattern. It is the most instantly recognisable of blue-and-white pottery, a style that came to dominate the English table for two hundred years or more and still casts an influence over our tableware. Behind its success lay the entwining of a romantic backstory with the growth of transfer printing: the mass-production of ornately designed pottery.

The Willow Pattern came to represent 'China' more than any other image. The first design, an oriental idyll, was by Thomas Minton in 1780, Spode added the bridge in 1810, and that brought the love story. Attempting to recreate the perfect Chinese porcelain inspired potters' experimentations for centuries, leading from delftware to Meissen. Europe was absolutely fascinated by China, but the love affair was based almost entirely on blissful ignorance. Europeans created for themselves a fantasy of the country, *chinoiserie*, that was impossible to judge against Chinese reality; it was lavish, corrupt, dangerous and exciting.

When I was a child, my parents kept a set of the Judge Dee books by Robert von Gulik (a Dutch diplomat with a particular interest in China). In one of the novels, *The Willow Pattern*, Dee becomes involved in the mystery of the Willow Abode. Three characters run across the bridge, the leading two eloping lovers, behind them chases the murderous father. These lovers originated in the story that had grown around the Willow Pattern, apparently an ancient Chinese tale, but in fact a nineteenth-century construction. At the right of every Willow Pattern is a temple and a little house: here Knoon-Shee, the love-struck maiden lover, has been held captive. Rescued by her true love, she crosses the bridge with him and they escape by ship to the island that sits at the top of each design. While they are asleep, her father catches up and burns them in their sanctuary. When the sun rises, two doves fly into the sky. The lover's spirits, together forever. In van Gulik's book, the story of the Willow Pattern was a red herring, a romance to distract from grim reality.

THE WILLOW PATTERN

Ironstone pottery
Probably Staffordshire
Nineteenth century

A MUDLARK'S TREASURES

MONTELUPO
MAIOLICA
1550–1600

There is a short paragraph in Helen Macdonald's book, H is for Hawk, *that describes precisely how I feel about mudlarking. She writes:*

I once asked my friends if they'd ever held things that gave them a spooky sense of history. Ancient pots with three-thousand-year-old thumbprints in the clay, *said one.* Antique keys, *another.* Clay pipes. Dancing shoes from WWII. Roman coins I found in a field. Old bus tickets in second-hand books. *Everyone agreed that what these small things did was strangely intimate; they gave them the sense, as they picked them up and turned them in their fingers, of another person, an unknown person a long time ago, who had held that object in their hands.* You don't know anything about them, but you feel the other person's there, *one friend told me.* It's like all the years between you and them disappear. Like you become them, somehow.

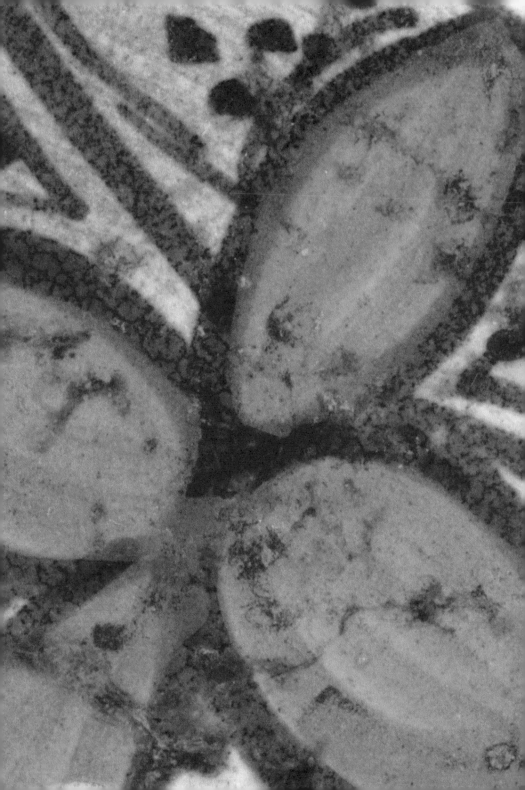

Small things are not great treasures. They do not make one rich, they do not even sit well on the mantlepiece, outside of a *wunderkammer*. But what they do give is an unparalleled, incredible, connection to individuals of the past. It is a deep and unsettling feeling, to place your thumb where a potter four hundred years ago placed his, to idly polish a stud button with your finger that hasn't been polished for a couple of centuries. The lightening-bolt bond that flashes between you and someone that history has otherwise forgotten satisfies, or arouses, emotions that typically lie dormant. It crystallises the human need to be connected with our forebears, is a form of animistic ancestor worship.

The objects in this chapter have lost their stories, but I love them all the more for that. They have hand-scratched patterns that can be languorously retraced, textures and equivalences that I find magical. Some are unusual, some rare. Others the most common find on the beach. The rhythmically combed glaze of the eighteenth- and nineteenth-century baking dishes (see page 139) is my most enchanting encounter, even though I see ten pieces every time I walk by the river. These pieces are the true fragments of London: international, local, beautiful. Completely human.

PLATTER

Surrey/Hampshire borderware
Seventeenth century

BAKING DISH

Combed glaze
Eighteenth or nineteenth century

Although these share a zig-zag pattern, they've been made in very different manners. The borderware platter (opposite) had slip poured over, the baking dish (above) had two colours of slip applied together and then intermingled with a comb. Combed glaze is common on the river, but full of character and one of my favourite finds.

BAROQUE PEARL

Freshwater
Undated

BACHELOR BUTTON

Base metal and glass
Late-eighteenth to early-nineteenth century

Both of these finds made me feel like a stereotypical treasure-hunter; in my mind when I found these I was throwing fountains of glistening jewels above my head and letting them pour down upon me like rain.

MONTELUPO
MAIOLICA

NORTH HOLLAND
SLIPWARE

Italy
1550–1600

I like very much that I have in my collection
a piece of original maiolica: delftware's
grandparent. The colours are so vibrant it's like
endless summer.

Netherlands
Late-sixteenth to early-seventeenth century

A love of delftware often goes hand in hand
with a love of slip. These two pieces are roughly
contemporaneous: the one made in sunny Italy,
the other in grey Holland. Maiolica is fresh and
light, slipware stodgy, heavy, satisfying on cold
winter days.

BOWL

TIN-GLAZED EARTHENWARE

England
Around 1800

Pearlware, the material that killed off delftware.
A very simple palette and extremely elegant
style of decoration.

Possibly North Italian
Late-seventeenth century

To me these look like a pair of staring eyes and
the bridge of a nose. The ferocious monobrow
completes an unsettling picture. It appears a
fragment of Picasso ceramic.

TRAILED SLIPWARE

UNIDENTIFIED

Seventeenth century

This is just the most gorgeous drip on the sweetest honey-coloured ground. Everything about this is edible. Except the object itself of course, which would be crunchy.

Undated

I can't identify this, yet the perfection of the curlicue makes it a valued find. While the curled drip of slip to its left is spontaneous and full of life, this twist of metal is all restrained elegance, a formal pirouette.

STORAGE JAR RIM

STORAGE JAR HANDLE

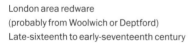

London area redware
(probably from Woolwich or Deptford)
Late-sixteenth to early-seventeenth century

London area redware
(probably from Woolwich or Deptford)
Late-sixteenth to early-seventeenth century

Both of these fragments would have come from similar jars, huge earthenware vessels probably used in brewing. What I love most about them is their visible thumbprints. It is possible to rest your thumb inside them and feel intimately connected to the potter who made this, and the brewers who last held it five hundred years ago.

Both types of thumbprints were decorative, but both also had structural importance in making large jars stable. On the left, the thumbing was on a band of clay applied to strengthen the rim of the pot (the glaze at the top is just visible). The thumbprints give a sort of triangular profile, and a triangle, as any engineer knows, makes a strong and lightweight support. In the photograph above, the potter's thumb was used to fix the handle securely to the jar.

SGRAFFITO WARE

Beauvais, Northern France
Sixteenth century

ROMAN GREYWARE

Undated

These two pieces of pottery look similar, yet they are separated by over a thousand years. Both show the way their potters explored the physicality of clay; the way it takes impressions and keeps them. This piece of greyware has been stamped and rouletted (with a shaped roller driven across the surface). Opposite, the potter scratched into the surface of the clay.

TESSERAE

Undated

MOSAIC

Nineteenth century

Because mosaics are so traditionally associated with Roman decoration, it's very easy to pick up any piece and assume it's 2,000 years old. Unfortunately, an individual tessera is extremely difficult (if not impossible) to date. A good chunk of mosaic can be dated by the mortar that sticks it all together.

INDUSTRY

COPPER RIVET

London is so lived-in today, so determinedly residential, that it is sometimes difficult to imagine it as an industrial hub, as much producer as consumer. London's industrial decline occurred slightly earlier than that of the northern powerhouses, but not remarkably so. It can be dated to the aftermath of the Second World War, when a combination of bomb damage, port closures and environmental regulation made Britain's futuristic industrial parks attractive alternatives. One of the objects I discuss in this section, a crucible from the Morgan Crucible Company (pages 158–9), exemplifies this: a company that had a profound impact on the Industrial Revolution, even on the geography of London, moved its operations to where land was cheaper in the second half of the twentieth century.

Sometimes, walking through parts of central London, one can still be surprised by the noise of panel beating and the smell of dangerously hot metal. Back streets in Southwark or Fulham are still home to industry. One can come across it suddenly in the midst of a residential area. It is only on reflection that we realise our surprise is the wrong way around, that the flood of housing was built for the workers at factories that are now unwelcome, vestigial intruders into a comfortable street. London was built on building, and it is all-too-much forgotten, even as the signs of its industrial history are seen everywhere.

The most obvious traces of industry are found in the architectural fabric. Firstly, the small areas of still-active factories; then, in the vast majority of them (where still standing) that have been converted to dwellings. Expansive lofts, tiny apartments owned by foreign capital: look up and see the towering windows that once lit workshops, the winches and the huge gateways for horse-drawn carts.

When I was renovating my own house, I found a bottle of Cannon Stout from the Second World War. Just as I now go down to the river when the tide is out, then, in the evenings when the builders were out, I used to lift up the loose floorboards and scout about with a torch for artefacts of my own ghost residents: leftover tiles from the hearths, still-full bottles of War Grade beer (whose stoppers were made with less material), a gas mask. My street, near a mainline railway, had been badly bombed. The Cannon Brewery, brewer of

'The Thames gave birth to the town and to its industries; a fast-flowing tidal river provides the power, transport and waste disposal that are essential to manufacturing.'

the bottle, was founded around 1720; it occupied an enormous footprint off St John Street, Clerkenwell. The site is now a mixture of medium-rise new builds and restoration, a home to architects and designers who enter by gates the brewer's drays would once have clip-clopped through.

The river is probably the next best memento of London's industry. It was the hub of it. The Thames gave birth to the town and to its industries; a fast-flowing tidal river provides the power, transport and waste disposal that are essential to manufacturing. Industrial infrastructure still stands on the Thames' embankments: cranes, wharves, the factories themselves. Where they don't make money for rentiers, they tend to be badly maintained; there is currently a campaign to save the last crane of Surrey Docks, the Red Crane of Odessa Wharf. Conserving industrial heritage has never been an easy sell. In part, I think, that's because for all the romantic nostalgia associated with manufacturing, it cannot be stripped away from the dirt and danger and sheer inhuman scale of the endeavours. Work in factories, for most of their history, has been an example of Thomas Hobbes' description of life without governmental regulation: nasty, brutish, and short.

London began its life as a trading centre. There is no real evidence for a substantial settlement before the Roman invasion; the archaeologist Martin Millett suggests that London was deliberately created to foster trade with the developing Roman province of Britannia by opportunistic Romanised traders from other provinces. The first Roman London was a planned city, the traders were neutral outsiders who could trade effectively with rival tribes. Besides the oysters and salt mentioned in *Pleasures of the Table*, Britain was also known for exporting dogs (a favourite was the British bulldog), wool and metal. Slaves from Caledonia (Scotland) and Hibernia (Ireland) were a major export.

It makes economic sense to build up industries around trading centres. Raw materials are easily available, and the journey from manufacture to merchant is minimised. As the most important centre in Britain, London developed unique and specialised industries. In many ways we see the same today: people want to move to London because that's where the exciting things are happening – be they in tech, finance or the arts. Specialist Roman craftsmen gathered in London, feeding innovations and manufacturing the sophisticated tools that workmen in the provinces could not make themselves. Metal forging, glass making and pottery were based in London and exported nationally; technical and luxury goods made here were sent throughout the empire. Where precision was required, manufacture tended to take place in London.

In the late-fourth century, Roman rule in Britain was under attack. By the early-fifth century Rome was no longer able to defend its province; when Rome was captured in 410, the Emperor Honorius let Britannia establish its own governments. In time, London fell into ruin. There is speculation that the romance of the fallen city proved a touristic draw for Saxons who would visit for the thrill of the desolation. This speculation comes from a single Saxon brooch, found in the Roman bathhouse at Billingsgate. Building materials of the city were stripped and reused.

In time, Anglo-Saxon Lundenwic returned to its position of mart of many nations (see Bede, page 109), continuing to grow under Danish rule. As under the Romans, the centralisation of the major market in London brought with it the formation of clusters of specialised industry. These were strengthened by the incorporation of guilds, groupings of industries and craftsmen to regulate quality and prices (and to keep out outsiders). Guilds were begun in Saxon London, but didn't reach full strength until the chartering of livery companies began after the Norman invasion.

The first known Royal Charter of the City also can be credited to the Normans. London had been afforded special privileges since Saxon folkmoots, but it was the 1067 charter that confirmed its rights. William the Conquerer fortified the city too, building Baynard's and Montfichet's Castles and the Tower of London to defend it. The first livery company to be chartered was the Weavers' Company, in 1155. More followed in the thirteenth century, including the Loriners (metal riding accessories like bridles and spurs), Cordwainers (shoemakers and leatherworkers), Fishmongers and the Painter-Stainers; it was the fourteenth and fifteenth centuries that saw the explosion of chartered companies, including many of the Great Twelve: the most important companies to London, as of 1515. At the top of the list is the Mercers' Company, the merchants' association. Five of the Great Twelve companies made things, the rest were specialised trade associations. But even if they weren't the most important companies for the city, industrial guilds were vital for bolstering each specialism. They also maintained the system of apprenticeships and training for young entrants to the trade. These were jobs for life; children would enter early and work inside their profession until they couldn't work any more.

R. Campbell's 1747 directory *The London Tradesmen* was a careers advice bible written to help those 'Parents of Youth' about to enter the job market. He describes in detail the activity of all possible trades in London and is careful in each instance to lay out not only the roles and responsibilities, but the expected wages. Some professions pay by a fixed rate, but many labourers were paid by the amount they produced. Corkcutters (*worth no boy's while to learn the mystery*) earned 'Eight Shillings a Week at so much a Dozen of Corks'; snuff-men worked 'at so much a Pound' (*the trade was abundantly profitable, but had become over-stocked*); and the Drawers on pottery (which requires the painter's genius and more, because the *Colours unburnt have not the least Resemblance to those produced by the Heat of Fire*) are paid by the 'Dozen of Pieces painted' and may earn from 15 to 30 shillings a week.

These trades operated in small factories, but change was coming. Campbell explains pin-makers' primitive assembly line, breaking down the activity into five separate roles. This was taken up by Adam Smith thirty years later (see pages 162–3), putting in place the economic theory behind the Industrial Revolution. And what a revolution it was for London. By the mid-nineteenth century, London was the largest manufacturing city in Britain by far, with almost 400,000 people employed in industry. The Industrial Revolution may forever be associated with the North of England, transforming a picturesque Eden into a Dantesque hell.

'The Industrial Revolution may forever be associated with the North of England, transforming a picturesque Eden into a Dantesque hell. . . . the revolution changed London even more.'

The town of my childhood, Stalybridge in Cheshire, was a bucolic valley with fifty pretty little cottages in the mid-eighteenth century. A hundred years later, Friedrich Engels described its overflowing mill-town streets as repulsive and shocking filth. But the revolution changed London even more.

In 1500, one in fifty Englishmen (women and children) lived in London, by the beginning of the eighteenth century it had grown to a tenth of the English populace and London was the largest city in the world. As the population grew, so did the borders of London. The cores of the City and Westminster extended tentacles towards each other, and then joined. In the first third of the nineteenth century, the population of the City decreased but districts to the north like Islington more than doubled in size. (The 2011 Census has only 7,400 people living in the Square Mile. The only approximation for the quietude of the Thames is walking in the City on a weekend.) Parts of the East End doubled, some parts trebled, so did the western suburbs of Kensington and Chelsea, although the East End had six times the population of the wealthy west.

Keeping London fed required produce from a 10-mile radius, sold in over thirty markets. Trades clustered densely, some around these markets, as can be seen in the animal bones on pages 164–5; streets maintained a commercial character for decades, then suddenly changed. Clerkenwell was known for watchmaking; Spitalfields for silk; in the late-nineteenth century Camden made most of the world's pianos.

'London's industrial past is nearly invisible to Londoners today. Even though the manufacturing might of the city has rivalled, sometimes dominated the Northern powerhouses of Manchester, Liverpool and Birmingham, historians have passed over this heritage.'

Just as the Romans chose the site of London because of the Thames, so the river became the centre of London's great industrial boom. London was the largest port in England, accounting for two-thirds of foreign trade. The City sucked in the capital of the world and redistributed it to industry through investment and consumption. Raw materials came into London through the Port, were transformed by industry, and exported internationally as finished goods. Furniture is an example of this. It was one of the largest employers (after metalworking and textiles) and mixed light and heavy industry. It all began with timber imported by river; saw mills and timber yards sprang up near the India Docks to process the wood. The most prestigious furniture makers ensured they had first dibs on the best wood from the colonies. For small firms, the East End was the centre of the trade; they bought timber with what money they'd made the previous week, then sold their wares to large retailers. It was an accessible entry for Jewish immigrants settling in Whitechapel. Warehouses dominated Curtain Road, showcases for wholesale and export: what arrived as lumber in West India Dock left again by the Port of London, sawn, shaped, polished.

London's industrial past is nearly invisible to Londoners today. Even though the manufacturing might of the city has rivalled, sometimes dominated the Northern powerhouses of Manchester, Liverpool and Birmingham, historians have passed over this heritage. The city has been seen as a base for merchants, traders, financiers: those money-makers and rent-keepers. Forgotten is the fact that London once had more steam power than Glasgow and Leeds put together. But industry is no longer at eye level in London. To see its traces you must look for it, in architectural remnants, or on Thames beaches, where the history is there for the taking.

CRUCIBLE

Morgan Crucible Company
Battersea, London
Probably twentieth century

A just-decipherable 'Morgan' reveals this fragment to be an important link to London's industrial heritage. It comes from the Morgan Crucible Company, a company that revolutionised the foundations of international industry and physically changed the profile of the River Thames. Crucibles are at the bedrock of all industry: they are the vessels used to melt metal.

The company was founded in 1856 by six Morgan brothers (from a family of ten) who had come to London from the Welsh village of Glasbury-on-Wye. They began as an import/export business, but one of the items they offered, an American crucible, was so successful they licensed the rights to make it. They opened a small factory in an old pottery works by the river in Battersea and called it The Patent Plumbago Crucible Co. Plumbago is graphite, not a variant of lumbago: the name means lead-like, from the latin *plumbum*.

The Morgans' crucibles had a dramatic impact on the purity and efficiency of their users' productions. Competitors' crucibles would shatter unpredictably from heat-shock. The Morgans', made from a mixture of graphite and ceramic, lasted longer, never broke, and according to an 1859 advert of theirs, saved 'more than 50 per cent in time, labour, fuel and waste'. By 1862 the crucibles were being used by the Royal Mint as well as the Mints of India, France, Russia and Australia.

The factory grew so much they embanked the river, bringing the works out over the foreshore mud. Their clocktower, Ted Morgan's Folly, became a feature of the view. Whistler painted it in *Nocturne in Blue and Silver* (1878), a dark reflection of the Thames now part of the White House collection.

The company diversified, first into making parts for electric motors that were used in trams and electric railways throughout the world. By the middle of the twentieth century Morgan components were found at the centre of a huge array of industrial operations. And then, in the 1970s, the company outgrew London and moved with romantic circularity back to Wales. The Battersea factory was demolished, even Ted Morgan's Folly. During my research, I realised that I once had dinner where the glowing clock had stood. It is now Richard Rogers' mountain of glass, Montevetro. The host, a Swiss banker.

Today, Morgan Advanced Materials is a vast corporation manufacturing everything from ceramic armour for military vehicles to parts for jet engines. They still make crucibles.

This is one of the few objects in my collection that would have impressed a nineteenth-century mudlark. It may look humble, but in this little copper rivet there was cash at the dolly's. True mudlarks, many of them children, unable even to afford rags to wear, would sell their finds to their dolly – the meanest of pawnbrokers, and consider it a good day's scavenging if they could make four pence. '8d was a jolly lot of money.' Henry Mayhew describes the infant mudlarks hanging desperately around shipbuilding yards:

> The mud-larks collect whatever they happen to find, such as coals, bits of old-iron, rope, bones, and copper nails that drop from ships while lying or repairing along shore. Copper nails are the most valuable of all the articles they find, but these they seldom obtain as they are always driven from the neighbourhood of a ship while being new-sheathed.

This rivet is from a clinker-built boat, a round-bottomed Thames wherry, as ubiquitous a taxi in its day as the black cab is now. For most of the city's history, the majority of navigation was done by river. Inland roads were chaotic and ill-kept and, until Westminster Bridge in 1750, London Bridge was the only road across the river. Better to thrust yourself into the dependable chaos of the water, the thousands of wherrymen, poaching fares, hollering and drunk, chained to their oars like galley slaves, according to Johnson. But they were licensed, just like taxi drivers are licensed: their badges are still found (by mudlarks with keener eyes than mine), and it's because of the wherries that we can get down to the shore at all. Watermen's stairs are just taxi ranks that get wet twice a day.

COPPER RIVET

Copper rivet and section of clinker-built boat
Eighteenth to nineteenth century

BRASS PINS

Undated

There was a smartly dressed man crouched over the beach, eyes down, back bent, a pose familiar on the foreshore. I walked over to see what he was spotting. 'Found anything interesting?' It's the mudlarker's 'caught anything today?' Curious, non-comittal. 'Well they are to me,' he said. 'You might not think so.' He looked up. In one hand, a pair of tweezers, in the other a baccy bag full of bristling wire. 'Pins,' he said, 'I find them architectural. There were ninety different types of pins in those days. And they're all uniquely bent. Beautiful.'

I like pins too. Picking them up is addictive, though I don't have tweezers. After each pin I say to myself, 'Right, that's the last one; save some for other people,' and then I spot another and before I know it I've pricked it through the cuff of my shirt and added one more to my improvised pincushion.

He told me he had eight baccy bags full of them and we spoke about Tudor women being fixed into their costumes (their dress was so elaborate, their maids pinned them in with hundreds of pins each morning). 'They were given pin money,' he said. '£50 a year. It was a lot in those days. Have you seen a £20 note?' He reached into a clip and pulled out a crisp twenty. 'Adam Smith, look,' he said. And there it was, I'd never noticed, Adam Smith in profile, an engraving of a manufactory, and this quote: 'The Division of labour in pin manufacturing (and the great increase in quantity of work that results)'.

I went home and looked up *The Wealth of Nations*. 'To take an example, therefore, from a very trifling manufacture . . .'. Smith uses pin-making to introduce the power that comes from the division of labour into specialised tasks. In his example, one man on his own could make twenty pins in one day. But break the processes down and in the same time ten men could make almost 50,000 pins. Thus Henry Ford and then Shenzhen.

One man draws out the wire; another straights it; a third cuts it; a fourth points it; a fifth grinds it at the top for receiving the head; to make the head requires two or three distinct operations; to put it on is a peculiar business; to whiten the pins is another; it is even a trade by itself to put them into the paper; and the important business of making a pin is, in this manner, divided into about eighteen distinct operations.

'There must have been a sewer once,' he said, pointing to the river wall. 'Pins fell off in the street and were washed out here.'

There has always been a standoff between the free-spiritedness of Southwark and the propriety of the capital on the north shore. London was a fiercely regulated place, with all manner of activities overseen by heavily controlling guilds. To make sure it stayed that way, all the fun activities were pushed across the river. There they clustered around London Bridge, the only dry route to the north. Everyone knows about the theatres, but the same applied to the other pleasures like bloodsports, drinking and sex. In particular, the stews, or brothels, brought in sufficient income to make taking them under control a consistently low priority. The most noxious and polluting industries also tended to be located south of the river: potteries, lime kilns, slaughterhouses, knackers' yards and tanneries.

There were repeated attempts to clear slaughterhouses from the City, such as the wholly unsuccessful 1488 Act passed to prevent the killing of beasts within the walls of London, but the area around Smithfield Market was thick with a cottage industry of slaughtermen. In his eighteenth-century survey of the town, John Entick wrote about a street near Newgate called Stinking-lane 'on account of the nastiness of the place occasioned by the slaughter houses in it'. But it was on the south bank that they were least effectively regulated.

Live animals and dead crossed the river for processing. In mediæval Southwark what wasn't wanted was dumped straight back in. It was illegal to do so, and it wasn't a practice that made the district popular, but Southwark was ruled by so many competing authorities – secular and ecclesiastical – that illegality flourished. By the nineteenth century there was a use for everything, blood, bones, fat and hair. In a survey of 1873 there are blood driers, scum boilers, tripe dressers and bone crushers. The giants in *The BFG* don't have worse names.

There are still a tremendous number of animal remains on the foreshore. In places, under Blackfriars Bridge is one example, the beach can resemble an ossuary. Vast shoulder bones and huge bovine molars lie alongside sheeps' skulls and the jaw bones of pigs. Remarkably, the smell has gone.

ANIMAL BONES

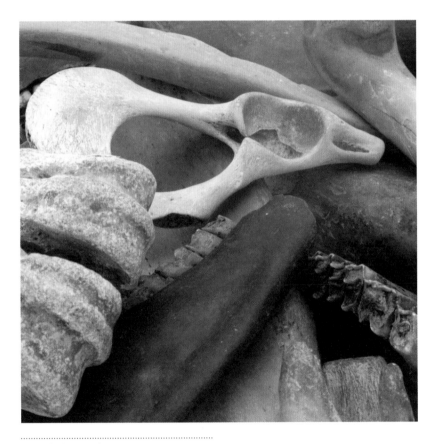

Probably nineteenth century

POLYCHROME DELFTWARE PAVEMENT TILE

1550–1650

This was the first important piece I found by the Thames. It's a polychrome tin-glazed floor tile – you can see just the touch of holly leaves and maybe even a berry up against the yellow in the top corner, and some intricate blue-and-white patterning lower down. The attraction of delftware floor tiles was short-lived for seventeenth-century Londoners. Their decoration quickly wore off, which made them spectacularly ill-suited to the job. It would have been like buying hand-painted silk wallpaper and laying it as carpet. So around the mid-seventeenth century, London potteries switched from making tiles for the floor to tiles for the wall: you can tell the difference because floor tiles are thick (about 15 millimetres) and wall tiles about a third of that.

I was so excited about this find that I brought it into the Museum of London, and there was introduced to the mudlarker's responsibility: reporting anything half interesting so that it can be recorded. The objects lying so casually on the beaches of the Thames are an important part, sometimes an astonishingly important part, of this country's history, and making sure that they're accessible for future research is vital. If you want to see the official record for this tile, search 'LON-A90670' online. I should imagine I visited that page five times a day for weeks after it was created, so proud was I at having found something Really Important.

This tile has some resemblance to tiles found during the excavation of the Rotherhithe pothouse, a pottery remarkable for occupying the site of an old moated royal palace. Sitting on the corner of Bermondsey Wall East and Cathay Street in Rotherhithe (and just down the road from Pottery Street) there are a few old stone walls sunk into municipal grass. These are what's left of the Inner Court of a palace built for Edward III between 1349 and 1356. Is it odd that a palace became a pottery? Well, archaeological evidence shows that before Edward had his palace here, there was a mediæval building, and before that Roman, and before that Bronze Age. Land carries its histories within it, and you build where there was a building before. It's safe, somehow, to start again where the human spirit has already conquered the wilderness.

I particularly like Mocha decoration. It wasn't a remarkable ware when it was made in the nineteenth century, but what's amazing is how it records a sort of chemical violence. The fern-like pattern is made by dropping acid onto the ground – the base colour – which is alkali: the reaction freezes into fractal fronds. Pottery is all chemistry; it's usually hidden, but Mocha captures it red-handed. With Mocha we're lucky that not only has the reaction been caught forever, but people who made it have also been preserved, thanks to a well-known Victorian author's trip to the Potteries.

In the early-1850s Charles Dickens got off the train in Staffordshire at what he describes as 'as dull and dead a town as any one could desire not to see. It seems as if its whole population might be imprisoned in its Railway Station'. He hates his hotel, despises its meat and drink, his 'pint of wine . . . tastes of pepper, sugar, bitter-almonds, vinegar, warm knives, any flat drinks, and a little brandy'. Sunk in misery, he engages his plate in conversation. It is an intriguing narrative device.

The plate foreshadows Mr DNA from *Jurassic Park*. It is cheeky and chirpy and probably dances around. It tells Dickens all about how pottery is made at the factory of his father, W.T. Copeland. It tells of flint reduced to a pap; of the potter making a teapot lid just by winking at a dab of clay; of the kilns, frightening like 'inverted bowls of a Pre-Adamite tobacco-pipe'. And after that, the plate says:

> I needn't remind you what a relief it was to see the simplest process of ornamenting this 'biscuit' (as it is called when baked) with brown circles and blue trees – converting it into the common crockery-ware that is exported to Africa, and used in cottages at home. For (says the Plate) I am well persuaded that you bear in mind how those particular jugs and mugs were once more set upon a lathe and put in motion; and how a man blew the brown colour (having a strong natural affinity with the material in that condition) on them from a blowpipe as they twirled; and how his daughter, with a common brush, dropped blotches of blue upon them in the right places; and how, tilting the blotches upside down, she made them run into rude images of trees, and there an end.

MOCHAWARE

Staffordshire
Nineteenth century

OCTAGONAL INK BOTTLE

Late-nineteenth century

Suddenly, it became important that the English public could read and write. There was a storm of reasoning behind it. Some wanted a more educated populace the better to fight wars intelligently. Others a more adept worker. Many felt an educated populace would be easier to control, cost the state less, and not fall into the clutches of the Workhouse. The Church set up Sunday Schools (guess who were reading the religious tracts on pages 38–9). For the children of the truly deprived, ragged schools offered a chance of education for the first time. By 1870 there were 250 ragged schools in London. School buildings were constructed, red brick, verdigris copper and imposingly tall. My son goes to one today with a vaulted assembly hall on the fifth floor at the top of a narrow spiral staircase described by Pevsner as 'romantically battlemented'. Even now the building is two or three storeys higher than anything around it. They were constructed to display the elevation expected of their new pupils.

In the 1960s Lawrence Stone came up with an intriguing way of charting the uptick of literacy in the nineteenth century using marriage registers. By comparing how many brides and grooms are able to sign their names on their wedding days, he was able cautiously to show that at the beginning of the nineteenth century, two thirds of men were literate and only half of women. Then, between 1840 and 1890, illiteracy was almost entirely wiped out. Men and women could actively participate in society.

Although fewer people could write than could read, the burgeoning citizenry needed means for written communication, at home, in school, at the office. At work, ranks of clerks swelled to keep pace with industrialised finance. Before PCs, clerks were computers – they were even known as such. Huge numbers of pen pushers and gallons of ink were required to perform basic accounting functions.

Cheap ink came in penny bottles like this, plugged with a screw of paper instead of a cork. Although beautiful (it's a really lovely octagon), the bottles were made so carelessly they were simply snapped from the blow-pipe to leave a jagged edge to the neck. It is broken by design, uncommon in fragments found in the Thames.

When I started rooting this out of the mud, my friend Josh and I convinced ourselves that it was an incendiary bomb. It's easy to frighten oneself on the foreshore. It's like being in a forest at dusk, far from anyone. The imaginative qualities of the mind come to dominate in empty spaces and shapes take on meanings, haunting, threatening. The thick beaches of Thames are the emptiest spaces in London; interstitial zones between the febrile activity of the banks and the joyriders of the river.

But a stoneware jar a bomb? There's no excuse, but our minds were unexploded arsenals. Such a thing wouldn't happen away from the Thames.

This was buried just east of Waterloo Bridge where the mud is thick and slippery and sometimes sinking steps caused me to remember the walk I took as a child across Morecambe Bay, and like then I felt miles from shore and vulnerable. The National Theatre stands ten metres above, thousands of people pass by every hour. Josh is eagle-eyed and knows more than I do about all sorts of things and has the persistence to email me with suggestions for identifications of the arcane long after I've relegated them to a shoebox. We often walked together. When the tide was low we would take unnaturally long lunch breaks and hope that nobody would notice the mud on our shoes when we got back to the office.

There is a feeling that I think is quite widely shared, that mudlarking is another way of walking; like walking in the hills, or by the sea, or exploring an urban environment. From this perspective the hunt is relegated to the periphery of our vision and instead we walk both to think and not to think. That by putting one foot in front of the other (doing so next to water helps) we can review our thoughts, empty unneeded ideas, recharge cognitive power. As our attention wanders we can be surprised by flashes of insight, and underfoot the gravel crunches on.

It is just as meditative when the hunt takes over, but directed outwards rather than in. Bent over a promising patch of shore I have no object in mind except to detect patterns in a random matrix of gravel, pebbles and junk. It is an activity that takes place entirely, inextricably, in the moment.

The bottle is a nineteenth-century ink jar; maybe a foot high. It would have refilled ink wells in schools and offices. The black mud I found it filled with was a simulacrum of its original contents.

BULK INK BOTTLE

Stoneware
Nineteenth century

GLASS CULLET

Undated

One of the things that I was most surprised to discover when I set up my Instagram account was the world of sea glass. I had no idea any such thing existed, and it was beautiful. Sea glass is a pebble of glass, worn smooth and round by the tumbling of the sea. It's frosted, as though it has been acid etched, and comes in a rainbow of colours. Since being introduced, I've found myself looking for it on stony beaches.

For a long time I assumed sea glass came from broken bottles, but I began to notice that some of the pieces were just too thick for a bottle. They were chunky lumps of glass and I couldn't work out where they could have come from. So I put the problem aside.

Then at a Thames beach I hadn't visited before, I picked up a large number of pieces of cullet. This scarlet-and-yellow one is the most spectacular, but I had ruby reds and amethysts and greens and blues. As I weighed them in my hand it occurred to me that, rounded, they would fit the dimensions of sea glass just perfectly.

Cullet refers to fragments of glass for reuse and recycling. It is primarily waste such as molten lumps that have fallen onto the floor and solidified, cuttings, moils (glass that encircled the blowing pipe) and shards. Where a glassworks made glass from scratch, it involved mixing raw materials with cullet and melting them together, but new glass can be made straight from cullet.

What was fascinating to me was the discovery in a study of historical glass edited by Koen Janssens that there was a sizeable mediæval market for cullet. Cargos of glass from the Levant were shipped to Europe – the raw manufacturing was done in Asia, the fabrication in Europe (sound familiar?). Shipwrecks line the Mediterranean and Adriatic with cargoes of the glass. Just off the coast of Venice, a sixth-to-eighth-century shipwreck held several hundred kilos of cullet.

With the widespread transport of cullet by sea, it seems to me quite possible that the sea glass being collected on today's beaches could in fact be hundreds of years old. Very much better than a broken bottle.

ANATOMY OF A POTTERY

No industry has left so many traces on the foreshore as pottery. Sure, there are bones from tanning, cullet from glass-making and coal from everything, but it is pottery that carpets the beaches most effectively. The reasons for this are many: besides location (all but one of London's delftware potteries were sited adjacent to the river), there is composition (pottery and flint have a similar density, so the hydrodynamics of the river tends to treat them similarly), endurance and sheer quantity. Pottery made its way into the Thames from industrial, commercial and domestic dumps. It was used by everyone, thrown away by everyone.

Pottery is also one of the few industries that allows the casual mudlark to recreate almost the entire industrial process from found artefacts, many of them as exquisite as finished pieces themselves. Above all the finer wares that came later, I treasure my discoveries of London delftware most. Delft is bold, naïve and sumptuously tactile (it is somehow both soft and brittle). Delftware also marks the point where London potteries became a force to be reckoned with: a national innovator.

White clay was brought in from Kent, Suffolk and Norfolk and mixed with stronger London clay. The clays were stored in a pond, before being sieved and mixed for use. Wet clay was thrown on a wheel using moulds or a former to get a uniform profile. Turners were paid piecework, so worked pretty quickly. Finished pieces dried on racks before their first firing – at which point they were called biscuit. The biscuit wares were dipped into a slurry of glaze (a mixture of traditional lead glaze with the addition of tin oxide – which made it white). The earthenware biscuit absorbed this glaze like a sponge, and when it had dried it was ready for decoration. Artists used cobalt blue, manganese purples as well as red, yellow, and green from iron, antimony, and copper. But even coated in tin-glaze, the biscuit was incredibly absorbent. Painters used pin-pricked templates to mark the outline of the design, but every stroke they used was there for keeps, which explains the dashing, vibrant, exciting decoration of delftware: it had to be impulsive. Once dry, the vessels were fired again and sold, at the time, as gallypots.

'Painters used pin-pricked templates to mark the outline of the design, but every stroke they used was there for keeps, which explains the dashing, vibrant, exciting decoration of delftware: it had to be impulsive.'

BISCUIT

Probably the base of a wet drug jar (used in
apothecary shops to hold syrups). A vessel
after its first firing.

VITRIFIED KILN WALL

This piece of kiln was exposed to the most intense heat of the fire, causing the silica within it to turn to a gorgeous glass.

SAGGAR

Also known as shigg, these pots, glazed in a
beautiful moss green, were made solely to hold
vessels being fired. A cylindrical saggar like
this would have held stacked plates, protecting
them from the flames.

TRIANGULAR HOLE AND PEG

Plates were stacked on the sharp end of
triangular ceramic pegs stuck through saggar
walls. This gave the smallest possible point
of contact between a plate and its support,
minimising the risk of the two sticking together.

TILES

POLYCHROME
TILE
LATE 16ᵀᴴ CENTURY

London is a city of tiles. Roofs, façades, porches, fireplaces, the littlest rooms, everywhere they are clad in beautiful warm ceramic tiles. Before the Great Fire, London roofs were tiled with deep red terracotta (they're found in great mounds in places on the Thames, dumped during the clean up); fifteen hundred years before then, similar red earthenware was also used by the Romans for their underfloor heating. Mediæval London was floored with patterned encaustic tiles — they can still be seen at Westminster Abbey, and floor tiles continued to be used with the introduction of delftware from Antwerp. Less hardy than encaustic, delftware began creeping up the walls, turning houses exquisitely blue and white.

Come Victorian London, tiles had conquered all. Terracotta tiles in complex moulds faced glamorous new developments in Chelsea, the terracotta a defence against London particulars, those thick brown smogs that left clothes and buildings sticky with cobwebs of soot. The Arts and Crafts movement filled every flat space with art tiles; the interwar years were tiles' last hurrah before they were pushed back to kitchen and bathroom. All of these tiles can be found by the Thames. We can tick off the centuries using tiles alone, and more than anything, their flat, fragmentary forms radiate beauty.

The Roman hypocaust tile (pages 224–5) is instantly recognisable thanks to the stripes they all carry. Hypocaust tiles are the sort of artefact that adds sardonic overtones to the question, 'What have the Romans done for us?'. Well, underfloor heating, for one. The remains of a London hypocaust can be seen *in situ* at the Roman bathhouse in Billingsgate. It's a fascinating compromise with history; part of the baths was discovered in 1848 when the Coal Exchange was being built on Lower Thames Street; the full site was excavated in the late-1960s, and then an early-1970s office building was constructed right over the top of it. It's one of London's most literal hidden treasures: walk down concrete steps into the basement of a City building and find yourself on suspended walkways above a private Roman villa. It's infrequently open, but a similar, more curated experience can be had at the Guildhall. Take the lift down to the level of the Roman street and step out into an amphitheatre.

Mediæval London is well represented on the Thames by roof tiles. Less often found are the unbelievably gorgeous floor tiles of the period. These heavy, fat slabs of earthenware were stamped with a pattern. Some were left in relief, the whole glazed with lead. Others had the indentation filled with white clay, the result a dusky brown base with sumptuous yellow designs of fleur-de-lys, or birds, or foliage, even figurative scenes.

Then came tin-glazing. The story of how adding tin oxide to a lead glaze to get a pure white glaze is told on page 179: the technology crept westwards and north from the Islamic world, reaching Flanders at the beginning of the sixteenth century and England fifty years later. Tin-glazed pottery, or delftware, introduced an explosion of colour into pottery, starting with tiles. Vibrant blues, yellows and greens could suddenly pop against a white background. A delftware pavement can still be seen in the chapel of The Vyne in Hampshire. Narrow avenues of elongated hexagonal tiles run in front of the pews and burst with colour and imagination: portraits, intricate designs, skulls and crossbones. Out with the old and in with the new. The tiles at

The Vyne were at the very forefront of fashion, imported from Antwerp. Soon England imported potters from there, too, starting with Jasper Andries in 1567, who set up a tile pavement pottery in Norfolk. Dutch potters began working in London a few years later. The tile on page 193 is probably one of theirs. It is a very early piece – it has some similarities to some at The Vyne – and it's one of my best-preserved tiles, in better shape even than some Victorian ones. The glaze on it shines as though it were fresh out of the kiln, the colours glow. I found it, sitting colour-side up, on top of a rock.

Floor tiles were thick, an inch deep or more, and the tin-glaze gave them an incredible lustre. It's a tactile glaze, sculptural in the way it chips and peels off the body, which makes it easy to identify on the riverbank. But tin-glaze wears, and it quickly wears out, particularly under the indelicate footwear of the seventeenth century, so around 1650 the fashion for tiles switched from the floor to the wall. Tiles became thinner (and thinner still, as time and technology passed) and the patterns and colouring stabilised. From the polychrome delights of the late-sixteenth century, seventeenth century tiles fell under the spell of the chinoiserie passion for blue-and-white, occasionally purple. Influenced by the high-status Chinese porcelain then being imported, the palette for potters was much reduced. But at the same time, the scope for decoration exploded dramatically: arcadian scenes filled the walls, as well as animal studies, religious stories, quotidian vignettes, naval battles. As much as I adore blue-and-white delftware tiles (and I do, more than almost anything), when they cover a wall the impression is like a strobe light, psychosis-inducing, tiles leaping from fisherman to flayed martyr to foxes in their dens all in a densely packed grid of imagery.

Then industrial tile-making supplanted the artisanal delftware potters, and tiles were everywhere. Not just restricted to those wealthy enough to afford hand-crafted walls, industrial tiles from manufacturers like Minton, Maw and Pilkington's covered Victorian London inside and out. From the Gamble dining room at the V&A, where you can sit and sip a cup of water for nothing at all and stare up at the crisp white columns, to the terracotta tiles at the Natural History Museum across the road, decorated with the animals of its collection. The 'suburban' houses (for which read Zone 2) that were thrown up by the railways had tiles in their doorways, on their hall floors, around their fireplaces, in kitchens and bedrooms. Tiles were as much a part of London's unstoppable expansion in the late-nineteenth century as the yellow London stock brick, turned black almost instantly by all the coal fires the new houses burned.

Most treasured of all Victorian tile makers was William De Morgan. De Morgan was part of the Arts and Crafts movement, whose principles centred around the return to making by hand, and his tiles are the most glorious, lustrous and vibrant of the period, with influences right the way back to the earliest Islamic tiles. One day in late summer I went to the Fulham foreshore especially to look for fragments of De Morgan's tiles. His final factory had been there, in Sands End, and I felt it likely that some fragments would still remain in place. The more time I had spent searching Thames foreshores, the more convinced I'd become that, although the great currents of the Thames send objects spiralling all over the place, most of them don't travel that far from home. A compacted layer of pottery I'd found out east corresponded, I thought (I still think), to one of the earliest delftware potteries. I think it was the contents of their dump sold for hardcore for a new set of stairs down to the river. It's possible to imagine the heft of the barrows pouring out broken biscuit in the exact same place five hundred years ago.

In principle, I am sensible when I go down to the river. I always look before I leap, I walk where ground is solid, and if it starts to sink underneath my boots I turn around and say 'No thank you very much'. But getting to the foreshore by the De Morgan works wasn't that simple. I started off by Imperial Wharf. This micro-city of anonymous, luxurious glass apartments and unshoppable shops, London's embodiment of Ballard's *Cocaine Nights*, stretches west along the river before turning into the less glamorous Townmead Road Estate, built

'I came to a ladder where the top three rungs were rusting away from the wall. I went up it, my boots heavy with claggy mud, and over the wall into an industrial estate dominated by Topps Tiles. The irony of the situation was not lost on me.'

right over the De Morgan factory. I climbed a ladder down to a small patch of gravel and headed towards Fulham, but the ground soon ran out and left me with a wide stretch of mud to pass. A tentative step forward saw my boot sucked in up to the ankle. The only way out was up into a building site (hard hats and high-vis required) *via* half-built scaffolding. My overweening, heart-pounding desire to collect a sample of De Morgan (the sense-obscuring rush of adrenaline that floods a treasure hunter when he or she thinks they're about to strike gold) forced me westwards *via* the only possible route, frightened balancing along a 30-metre stretch of horizontal scaffolding pole and jumping the last stretch of mud to a shale bank. Thank God for Saturday-morning parkour classes with my five-year-old son. That shale soon brought me to another little estuary of mud, with a tiny strip of semi-solid ground just at the level of low tide, solid enough that it covered only the toes of my boot, and as I walked, I knew that every route behind me was closing off, the tide coming in over my causeway, the scaffolding unconscionable in reverse. I walked over two or three more banks, and two or three areas of mud, each time feeling ratcheted forwards. I tried to concentrate on finds when the ground was solid enough, but excitement had turned to claustrophobia (on a river bank in the middle of the largest city in Europe). There was a lot of Victorian detritus, but nothing from De Morgan. On the other side of Wandsworth Bridge I came to a ladder where the top three rungs were rusting away from the wall. I went up it, my boots heavy with claggy mud, and over the wall into an industrial estate dominated by Topps Tiles. The irony of the situation was not lost on me.

Tiles of ravishing artistry continued to be mass-produced through the early-twentieth century. Art Nouveau architecture found particularly successful use for the sinuous organic forms achievable in ceramics. Tube-lining (see page 194), the technique of pouring a thin raised bead of slip to separate areas of glaze, made it possible to explore new forms relatively cheaply, and to ensure depths of colour. In many ways it takes from the technique of enamelling: separating powdered glass with precious metals. The relation between glaze and glass is close: glaze is vitrified in a kiln, made glass-like. Art Deco kept the colours of Art Nouveau, added some new ones, and turned the serpentine lines into jagged angles, but with the advent of modern architecture, tiles faded into the background. They became utilitarian, at best broad abstract mosaics rising above Brutalist plazas, at worst a splash-back. I find it very pleasing that red terracotta tiles, hundreds of years old, massively outnumber these late-twentieth-century tiles on the river bank.

PEARLWARE PLATE

DELFTWARE TILE

Early- to mid-nineteenth century

This was the first piece of traditional blue-and-white delftware tile that I'd ever found. Much later, when researching this book, I was discussing it with an expert and he held it up in profile. 'Look,' he said. 'It's curved, not flat. And it's pearlware, not earthenware. And it's printed, not painted.' So very much not a delftware tile. But it is a wonderfully sensitive depiction of an alert sheep's hindquarters, which goes very well with . . .

Mid-eighteenth century

. . . this incredibly idyllic portrayal of sheep at rest. The perfect arcadian scene, with sheep in the background drinking from a fountain and the cud-chewer lying on soft grass in front. It is from a Golden Age, full of contentment and plenty, that could have been inspired by Virgil.

DELFTWARE TILE

DELFTWARE TILE

Mid-eighteenth century

Mid-eighteenth century

Manganese is a much rarer tone on a delftware tile than the exquisite cobalt blue. I like it for being unusual, but also the purple gives tiles at once richness and a stark, austere, contrast. This arm is probably from a biblical scene. Although it could be a farmer.

For all their variety, delftware tiles tended to be created within certain well-established frameworks. A central motif, sometimes contained within a circular vignette, and then a delicate decoration in each corner. This one is called the spider's head, for reasons that elude me; a more common corner decoration is known as the ox-head, a visual rhyme I find similarly opaque.

Mid-eighteenth century

Mid-eighteenth century

This fingernail-sized fragment shows either a farmer outside a long barn or a Chinese figure in an oriental scene. What I love about it is how it demonstrates the way in which the most naïve and casual brushstrokes capture emotion, hint at stories, and convey depth.

Quite a late tile, it stands in contrast to the figure adjacent. The brushstrokes are so much more confident; the turbulence of the waters powerful and threatening. It also shows the nail hole, where, while the clay was still leathery, the tile was cut to shape.

DELFTWARE TILE

ENCAUSTIC FLOOR TILE

Late-sixteenth to early-seventeenth century

Walking on tiles is such a sensual experience, they combine the softness of wood (unless you drop anything on them) with the weight of stone. It's hardly surprising tile pavements have always been popular, especially when they're as lustrous as this.

Nineteenth century

Victorian encaustic tiles are just as thrilling. They gave entrance hallways incredible drama: open the door and experience the geometry. My house lost its, possibly through bombing; when I walk down the street and see extant floors through open doorways I feel great pangs of envy.

DOORWAY TILE

TUBE-LINED TILE

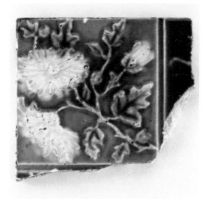

Late-nineteenth to early-twentieth century

What our house still has is its doorway tiles. Ours are pears; the other houses on the street cover most of the rest of the grocery aisle. The horticulturalists who follow my Instagram gallery confidently identify the flower as chrysanthemum.

Late-nineteenth to early-twentieth century

An exquisitely cropped tube-lined tile, where an outline of slip allows for crisp segmentations of colours. The sharp angles here would have made for some very stylish roses.

HEARTH TILE

HEARTH TILE

Late-nineteenth to early-twentieth century

Late-nineteenth to early-twentieth century

Although these are both hearth tiles I've mainly included them for their resonance with the most important tiled buildings in Victorian and early-twentieth-century London: pubs and Underground stations.

The perfect green (left) instantly denotes care and comfort, is almost an emblem of London. This delicate aqua blue is much more homely.

ADORNMENT

Although the mud of the Thames is a great preserver, it tends not to keep soft cloths and materials. Sometimes a few threads are found tightly wrapped around something metal. With accessories, however, the beaches are bounteous. Leather keeps well, and it is not uncommon to find entire shoes, almost wearable bar the mud they carry. Once they've dried out, they're like a child's shoes after a trip to the sandpit. More often one finds soles, with rows of hobnails like a shark's maw. Most common of all are the pieces of metal that held clothes together: buttons, dress hooks, buckles and pins remain when garments have long since disintegrated. Rings, brooches and other pieces of jewellery are there to be found too, though not often: they're treasure after all, and finding them demands suspense, frustration and a great climax of joy.

For me, these objects reveal a conflict about the way we choose to present ourselves to the world. At first glance, jewellery, accessories, seem foolish, superficial. No more than vanity. And yet, in the river at least, they are what is left behind. When all humanity before us has been swept away, forgotten, their names said for the last time many ages ago, when even bones are lost, what remains of people are their buttons. Perhaps the human attachment to trinkets, then, comes not solely from the desire to impress, but also from a need not to be forgotten. We cannot take them with us, and they are what remain to tell the stories of our passions, connections and affections.

There is a type of finger ring called the posy ring that embodies this. From the mediæval period until the eighteenth century these little gold rings were given as wedding rings or as tokens between lovers. I've never found one, but they're common enough. Their romance is hinted at in the name: posy comes from the word *poesy*, an old form of 'poetry', and each one of the rings was inscribed with a meaningful verse or motto. Some lines were chosen by the grand lovers, others were bought ready-inscribed from a goldsmith who kept a stock of them. Today we've got carousels of keyrings engraved with common names, then there were rings with phrases like, 'my hart is yovrs' or 'In love abide till death devide'. Perhaps sentimental, but love has room for sentiment.

Some of the jewellery will have made its way to the river *via* the sewers. Every householder has stood over a sink trap or a loo and wondered, 'Is it

'When all humanity before us has been swept away, forgotten, their names said for the last time many ages ago, when even bones are lost, what remains of people are their buttons.'

worth it?' But it's a small percentage, because most of the time the answer is yes. Sometimes you've just got to hold your nose. Or it might have dropped right into the river, from a wherry or bridge. And yet, just as a ring was given as a romantic gesture, so too were they cast away. This is the gothic romance, because it wasn't just in Wodehouse that one might return the ring. There is rejection, repulsion, fear. A spurned lover might cast it with tears from the bridge, watching their hopes fall with the warm metal. There is tragedy, too, the all-too-common suicide. The Victorians were fascinated with women killing themselves, particularly prostitutes, a grim play on their 'fallen women' soubriquet. *The Bridge of Sighs*, Thomas Hood's elegy, epitomises the genre: 'Past all dishonour, / Death has left on her / Only the beautiful.'

I suppose it is these thoughts of historic deaths, and their relation to the objects that I find today, that I find most unsettling about glibly picking pieces of costume out of the mud. Because it is *glorious*. When I find a nice dandy button I snatch it jealously from the shore. Suddenly it is mine, it is my precious. And yet the discovery provokes a not uncomplicated chain of considerations, once the euphoria has died a little. (A note on the hedonic treadmill that is mudlarking: each find elicits immediate joy, to be quickly nullified at the fear of missing out on the next one. The 'oh my, this is amazing but I want more' of the dirty urban treasure hunter.) On pages 164–5, the bones of Southwark, I wrote about how the wretched trades and the visceral pleasures were forced onto the south side of the river. It was a place where vice was sanctioned for prim City folk to enjoy themselves in daylight, but they took themselves back to North London at night. As dark fell, they were followed back over the bridges by vagabonds, cutpurses and worse.

Night was a dangerous time in London, right up to the end of the nineteenth century. Before the establishment of a regular police force in 1829 by Sir Robert Peel, it could be a free-for-all of casual bloodshed. Steven Pinker has long been making the argument that ceding the monopoly on violence to the state has been a major factor in bringing down the murder rate, that today is less violent than the world has ever been. He says that homicide in Western Europe has fallen by somewhere between 10 and 100 times since 1300 (110 homicides per 100,000 people in fourteenth-century Oxford to less than 1 per 100,000 in twentieth-century London). London is very safe. For most of the city's history, however, life was exceedingly cheap. Leaving the security of one's home at nighttime risked not just mugging, but death and the disposal of one's body in the river. Old London Bridge, the only way over the Thames, was a street with houses on either side, and between the houses were narrow openings onto the river. The piers of the bridge created vast turbulence, ferocious enough to ensure the death of almost everyone who fell, and a not uncommon way of settling a grudge was the unseen shove off.

Body after body hit the water. They washed up on beaches and were remarked upon (Pepys noted one body four days old) but were left untroubled to wash away again. Once the body and the clothes had gone, all that was left in the water was that which did not rot. So when I pick a button up with the jolt of adrenaline any finder feels, whose button am I finding? On pages 206–7, I imagine that my pile of buttons comes from the cashiering of the dishonourable, but I know that I am telling myself fairy stories, choosing dishonour before death.

But there are some items of adornment that have a happy ending. One story (in stories, I think, mudlarks resemble fishermen too) I was told was about a diamond ring, found by Queen's Stairs in front of the Tower of London. It was apparently a spiky Tudor beauty, extremely rare and undoubtably valuable, perhaps precious enough for royalty. The stairs take their name from Elizabeth 1's entrance to the Tower four years before she was crowned. It was not a happy arrival: Queen Mary had her sent there, and a trip to the Tower was usually one-way. On 18 March 1554, the first attempt to imprison her was foiled by a turning tide, and it wasn't until the next day that she was brought to Tower Wharf. Foreseeing her future, shaken by the suspense, Elizabeth dropped her mask for the one and only time and panicked. She refused to leave the barge. In 1563, John Foxe described the scene in his *Book of Martyrs*: 'We first have to consider in what extreme misery, sickness, fear, and peril her Highness was . . . being fetched up as the greatest traitor in the world . . .' before quoting Elizabeth as saying, as she finally leaves the barge, 'Here landeth as true a subject, being prisoner, as ever landed at these stairs.' In this distress, the story goes, is it not conceivable that she dropped a diamond ring from her wringing hands, to be found hundreds of years later?

I haven't been able to trace the ring, nor even the origin of the story, but even so, to discover something that could tell a story not of death in the river but ultimately of great glory gives hope to the other finds.

When I was researching the jewellery I have found in the river, I was introduced to Geoffrey Munn, Managing Director at Wartski, the famous old family jewellers just off Bond Street. (He's also well-known as an expert on *The Antiques Roadshow*.) It turned out he also kicked around the foreshore for artefacts. After we had discussed our finds, he stepped into a back room and returned with jewellery cases. One was a diamond tiara of Queen Victoria's, designed for her by Prince Albert. He opened a book he'd written, *Tiaras: A History of Splendour*, and showed me her wearing it in a picture by Winterhalter in 1842, and another from 1874, by Henry Richard Graves. It was the tiara she had worn on her first public appearance after her mourning for Albert, the subject of Theodore Bonnet's *The Mudlark*. We had come full circle, like a mediæval posy ring, which are, of course, sold by Wartski.

Geoffrey has had a love of discovery since childhood, when he longed to find a clay tobacco pipe but grew up where they're as rare as hen's teeth. Then, walking by a Thames embankment, he saw a pipe bowl on the shore below. He made his way down, picked it up, and became a mudlark. He lives by Lambeth Bridge, and can slip on his wellies whenever he sees the tide is out. Specific to that foreshore, he has an interest in three things: twelfth-century jug bases (which are bizarrely clustered there), Kangxi porcelain, which would have been imported from China during the reign of James I (and, given that the shore is almost directly under the Palace of Westminster, could well have fallen there from the hands of his courtiers) and, lastly, fragments of masonry with mediæval moulding, from the Palace itself. I joined him one morning and picked up a piece of each: the masonry is on pages 36–7.

With the tide coming in on the Westminster foreshore, we went across the bridge to Geoffrey's flat for breakfast. Here the circle of coincidences expanded to bring in other thinkers about the river. When we came out of the lift and stood before his window over the Thames I was sharply reminded of Iain Sinclair's visit in *Lights Out for the Territory* to the apartment of Lord Archer (Jeffrey, not Geoffrey. There is a pointed distinction between the two spellings), in Alembic House almost next door. Except, where Sinclair encountered a patronising PA and an absent host, I got generosity of knowledge and scrambled eggs and sausages. Yet the resonances were disconcerting, as when Geoffrey took out a small nineteenth-century oil of the view of the Houses of Parliament across the river as they appeared almost from his window (Sinclair went to Archer's flat to compare the view to pictures by John Bellany and Oskar Kokoschka). To complete the palimpsest, Geoffrey quoted from his chair by the window the lines of Wordsworth that also appear in *Lord Archer's Prospects*, 'The river glideth at his own sweet will. . . . And all that mighty heart is lying still!' To take from Sinclair, 'the Thames was everything'.

Stamped WB
Eighteenth century

'At Mr Jervas's, my old barber, I did try two or three borders and periwigs, meaning to wear one; and yet I have no stomach for it . . .'

Samuel Pepys, 9 May 1663

'I home, and by and by comes Chapman, the periwig-maker, and my liking it, without more ado I went up, and there he cut off my hair, which went a little to my heart at present to part with it; but, it being over, and my periwig on, I paid him £3 for it; and away went he with my own hair to make up another . . .'

Samuel Pepys, 2 November 1663

The periwig (or peruke, or just plain wig) found its place on the Englishman's head around 1660, when Charles II returned from exile in France in a ravishing swirl of fashion and luxury. The Restoration saw England eager to swap the Commonwealth's dour sensibilities for the joyous opulence of French style. Pepys' diaries catch the country at the inflection point: he withstood the trend for six months, then wore a wig for the rest of his life.

At first, wigs were worn only by the aristocracy, but they rapidly became an essential part of any man's dress, from gentlemen to artisans. Eighteenth-century men dressed with an incredible feeling for self-expression, the smallest item of their costume indicating taste, symbolism or allegiance. Their costume was high maintenance, and none more so than the full-bottomed wig, a hairpiece that stretched well below the shoulder. Every curl had to be wrapped around heated wig curlers like these, they left a lovely crisp shape on removal. Curlers were made of pipe clay, probably by just a few pipe manufacturers. Ones stamped WB have been found from London to America. Wigs rose, and then they fell. They became the victims of satire: in 1761 Hogarth published a print of them arranged taxonomically, *The Five Orders of Periwigs,* where he gave to wigs the (self)-importance the great architectural theorists of the day gave to Palladio's five orders of classical architecture. The simplest order is the Episcopal, the most ornate the *Queerinthian* (a pun on Corinthian and a homosexual slur used two centuries before it is thought queer began to mean gay). By the late-eighteenth century wigs slipped from fashion, helped along by a tax on hair powder. Eventually only the old and conservative wore them; young men became Romantics and let their hair blow free in the wind.

There could be a great secret hidden within this brass RAF button. A secret that helped tens of thousands of Allied soldiers to escape their prisoner of war camps and find their way to safety. The first reason I have my suspicions about this button is that it looks completely innocuous and ordinary. The other reason is that it rattles when I shake it.

It's an elegant button, made by the sensibly named Buttons Ltd. of Birmingham, and dateable to before 1952 by virtue of the King's Crown above the eagle. The size (23 mm, which is surprisingly large and heavy) makes it a tunic button. It would have shared the sternum with five other buttons looking exactly the same. But I don't think the others would have rattled.

I think this button rattles because it's hiding a compass, concealed inside one button of every RAF uniform to help prisoners of war escape.

The compass button was invented by Christopher Hutton, the genius of MI9, which was set up to help troops evade capture or escape if they hadn't managed to do the evading. Where Bletchley had mathematicians, MI9 had magicians. And as if the story couldn't be any more fantastical, it all began with Hutton losing a bet with Houdini just before the First World War. Hutton challenged Houdini to escape from a packing crate made in his uncle's Birmingham lumber yard. Houdini accepted, bribed the man making the crate, and won a well-publicised £100. When it came to recruiting for the newly formed MI9, the Head remembered the Houdini story and had Hutton called in.

Besides the compass button, Hutton developed maps printed on parachute silk (hidden inside Monopoly boards); escape boots (with saws in the laces and a file in the heel); and a fountain pen airgun. When the Germans discovered the hidden compasses, Hutton reversed the screw thread in the buttons. When the guards caught on to this, Hutton sent every airman out with a magnetic razorblade that would always point north when dangled from a thread.

This button won't unscrew. Not in either direction. Sixty years in the Thames has sealed it tight. But when I hold it to my ear and shake it, I know it will be there for me in an emergency.

RAF TUNIC BUTTON

Probably Second World War

BRASS BUTTONS

Eighteenth or nineteenth century

Men's costume in the eighteenth century was elegant, refined and as subject to swinging fashions as today's. Rakish silhouettes changed only gradually, but the position, quantity and purpose of a gentleman's buttons changed like the passing seasons. Buttons developed meanings: where they sat, whether they were open or closed, even if a buttonhole was blind or working. A casual flicker of the eye over a man's coat and that's him pigeonholed.

Large brass buttons like these, probably polished or gilt, quickly spread from the aristocracy to their servants. These bigger buttons were mainly worn above the waist, sitting in extravagantly decorated buttonholes on a gentleman's surtout (or great coat), his coat (with the lower orders and the military wearing double breasted), or his frock or waistcoat. A malacca cane was carried by means of a ring hooked over a coat button; I imagine it was always ready to trip up the unwary, like a stick stuck between the spokes of a bicycle.

The most important proto-gentlemen's club was even called Button's Coffee House, founded by the acerbic essayist Joseph Addison. It was the Shoreditch House of the eighteenth century. All the Georgian wits met there: Alexander Pope, Hogarth, Jonathan Swift. Although named after an actual Button (Daniel, the owner), Addison found much to enjoy with the physicality of the brass variety. His characters are often button-holed (though he doesn't use the term) – caught by the button by some bore. Buttons signify status all too well, even sarcastically: a man wearing 'a threadbare coat with new buttons' (and therefore a person of great worth) is appointed to sit on a fictitious Court of Honour adjudicating on matters such as 'Whether a man may put up with a box on the ear received from a stranger in the dark?' and 'How a man should resent another's staring and cocking a hat in his face?' (to which I would answer: no and all the resentment).

What then if the defendant was found guilty in the Court of Honour? I like to imagine they would have been cashiered: on the parade ground their swords would have been broken over their commanding officer's knee. On the steps of their club, their buttons torn from their jackets. The ultimate disgrace. With all the emphasis on honour there was amongst the dandies, it might explain why so many big brass buttons were washed off the streets and into the Thames.

These little gems have an icy intensity. In tone they remind me of glacial caves photographed in the *Natural Geographic* style (sharp as a blade, saturated like technicolour). In some way they epitomise the joy of finding fragments: that the wonder of an object is magnified in inverse proportion to its size. And nothing could be smaller than the littlest blue glass jewel: you could fit half a dozen of them on a penny with room to spare.

It's hard to date a cut-glass jewel, removed from any context. Techniques for shaping gems have been around since the Bronze Age, the same epoch that the earliest glass jewels, mainly beads, were made. Beads were extremely high status objects until Roman glass blowing technologies transformed them into a common and useful item to trade. Their value as trade was rediscovered when European countries began to stake out their empires. They were cheap to make but had significant costs for their destination markets, buying as they did the exploitation of human and mineral resources across West Africa.

Bohemian (i.e. Czech) glassmakers began cutting glass gems around the same time. There are exquisite examples from the sixteenth century in the Cheapside Hoard – that treasure-hunter's dream, discovered in 1912 by builders digging up a cellar in the City. Who doesn't hope against hope that they'll catch sight of something glistening when they take up a floorboard? Cut glass was seen as an augmentation to jewels like diamonds, rubies and sapphires. If not used interchangeably, they were at least worn by the same people. Paste, a leaded glass that could be cut to look almost exactly like diamond, was invented in France in the eighteenth century, and quickly spread to England. Aristocrats loved to dot themselves with paste. When travellers were genuinely afraid of murder by highwaymen, paste gems were used like the decoy $50 tourists used to carry for New York's muggers.

So these jewels could be Tudor, but it's much more likely that they are Georgian or Victorian, when everyone who was anyone wore glass.

CUT-GLASS JEWELS

Eighteenth or nineteenth century

SINHALA SURAYA

Sri Lanka
Probably twentieth century

In an odd spot by the abutment of a bridge, where I hadn't really found anything and didn't expect to, I picked up a tarnished brass tube. Later, cleaning it, one end moved a fraction of a millimetre. I stepped back and waited for the genie and my three wishes (world peace, a big house in the country and *an infinite number of wishes*). No genie. I wiggled and jiggled and levered the tube and eventually it opened. Something tightly wound was just sticking out. As I teased it away and unrolled it (just a fraction) my heart entirely forgot to beat. A copper scroll covered in arcane script. A new dead sea scroll. Dr Dee's lost cipher. I felt the omnipotent triumph of the tomb raider.

It was in perfect preservation, the copper shining like new, barring a few discolourations where the Thames had washed inside. Each symbol had been finely engraved by hand with a stylus, they sat inside a grid of peculiar geometry. Research suggested a takrut, a Buddhist talisman that looked intriguingly similar; I started emailing details to every South East Asian specialist at soas. The result? It was written in Sinhala, one of the official Sri Lankan languages and the link with London: Sri Lanka was once the British colony of Ceylon. From the end of the Second World War to the late-1960s, a large number of Sri Lankan professionals emigrated to the UK, surging after the 1962 Commonwealth Immigration Act, declining with a restrictive 1968 act, the year of Enoch Powell's 'Rivers of Blood'. And it was a retired Sri Lankan doctor and his wife who helped me to understand the significance of the scroll, known in Sinhala as a *suraya*. Sitting with them over Ceylon tea, Mrs Silva explained the scroll would have been written by a *gurunanse*, a Buddhist teacher or healer. Each symbol was an individual letter referring to a word in a holy stanza; only the *gurunanse* would be able to interpret the meanings they contained.

The *suraya* is worn by a believer to ward off sickness, death or misfortune: or contrariwise to help in examinations or gaming. It's hung from a chain around the neck or upper arm, the wearer must cleanse themselves each time they put it on, and have to take it off before engaging in activities like eating pork or beef, going to a funeral or having sex. In Sri Lanka, the practice is dying out. The younger generations no longer have much faith in the magical power of the talisman.

A sparkling body is just as important as sparkling buttons; the way we keep our teeth attests to that. Ancient Egyptians fashioned a tooth powder from mint, salt, pepper and dried iris. Chinese used bamboo and horsehair as a combined brush and toothpick. But the modern toothbrush didn't take off until John Bull's teeth began rotting brown and bloody thanks to cheap West Indian sugar. Cometh the hour, cometh the man. And this fragment of a bone toothbrush is the instrument that lets me tell the story of that man and of a great sectarian uprising: the Gordon Riots.

In 1778 Parliament passed the Papists Act, ostensibly a generous move to allow Catholics more freedom to enter public life. In fact, the government wanted to enlist fearsome (but unfortunately Catholic) Scottish Highlanders to fight the Americans in their War of Independence. The Papists Act meant these Scots could join up without swearing a hated anti-Catholic Oath of Allegiance.

Parliament got their Royal Highland Emigrants, but the regiment came at a price. In 1780 rumours spread across London that the act was cover to put Catholics in power, that a Catholic army was ready to take the streets. A Protestant petition and rally led by aristocrat George Gordon turned into a Kristallnacht, with 60,000 people destroying Catholic chapels, homes and businesses, burning their possessions in great bonfires. When prisons were burst open and fired, the riot turned into armed insurrection with hundreds killed. Victims and rioters alike were from the new middle classes.

One of the rioters, suspected, was William Addis, a stationer to the book trade. In the great accounting that followed, he was either forced into hiding in a friends' slaughterhouse or gaoled in Newgate Prison (accounts differ). Either place gave him access to bone and bristles: Addis' genius was to combine the two into a prototype toothbrush; bristles glued into simple holes drilled in a piece of bone. Later, at liberty, he commercialised the process and sweet-toothed Georgians adopted his invention in droves. It made him rich; his company, now known as Wisdom, still makes toothbrushes.

BONE TOOTHBRUSH

After 1780

Rowlands Drug Stores
1892–6

Lower Marsh, near Waterloo, has always been a high street of the sort we dream about. Apparently ignored by municipal zoning, there is no homogeneity of estate agents and chain restaurants and bookies. Once cat meat sellers sat side by side with textile wholesalers, and the pub The Spanish Patriot (named after the Spanish Americans during the French/Spanish wars of the early-nineteenth century) lorded over all. Everything was catered for.

No. 36 Lower Marsh started as one of the most respectable premises on the street. Until the outbreak of the First World War it was firmly medicative: first surgical and then pharmaceutical. In 1842, when it appears in the earliest street directory, it was the clinic of surgeon George Buckley Crowther. Lower Marsh seems to have been his first practice: he got his certificate from the Apothecaries Hall in April 1841, and had married Philippine Schilling five months later. In 1848 he passed the practice on to a new surgeon, Ellis Wilson, who shared the rent with a chemist (another Ellis: William Ellis Scrivener) – signalling the first major change of occupation. The Scrivener Ellis took over the premises the following year, and 36 Lower Marsh remained a chemist's for another sixty-three.

Edward Edisbury Rowland (of [Ro]wlands Drug Stores) was the third of the chemists, and the shortest-staying occupant. Scrivener had been there for ten years; his successor Jonathan Fallowfield spent thirty-one at no. 36. Rowland only lasted four years, between 1892 and 1896. Fallowfield was one of the pioneers of popular photography and so successful in retailing it the name Fallowfield & Co. was bought out and moved to Charing Cross Road. Rowland promoted himself as a 'photographic chemist' (as well of course as a maker of toothpaste that sweetened the breath without injuring the enamel). The chemist who came after Rowland, W.J. Green & Co., reverted to chemist (plain old), and lasted fifteen years. His was the last pharmacy at no. 36.

During Green's reign, clothing makers and retailers had been steadily increasing in number on Lower Marsh. When he left, they moved into no. 36. First Pauline Owen, a milliner and linendraper, then Cohen brothers, linendrapers and later milliners. The last occupant was Miss M. Swyers. She – can you guess it? – was a milliner. And a costumier. In the Second World War the entire block was destroyed. Post-war the vacant lot was occupied by a greengrocer. And then in 1950 modernity arrived. The American Trussed Steel Concrete Company built their English headquarters, Truscon House, there, using their own flagship technology. That building still stands. It's now the head office of Christian Aid.

INDULGENCES
AND COMFORTS

ARMAND MARSEILLE
BISQUE DOLL
MOULD 370
1894 – 1920s

Perhaps the most poignant pieces to find by the river are objects that were once loved and played with. Things that were frivolous, not utilitarian. You can, I think, tell a lot about a people by the way they choose to entertain themselves, with what they seek solace. In the act of choosing, people reveal their characters or culture. Two dolls of a similar age that I have exemplify, for example, the economic disparity of London. They're both German, both made of bisque, a sort of liquid clay that can be perfectly moulded. The one, a fragment of a head, was expensive and expressive, it would have had glass eyes, silken hair and beautiful clothes (pages 230–1). The other, the size of a couple of joints on my little finger was the very opposite: static, white, frozen. It would have cost a penny or two (pages 232–3). Together, they make the social differences between the two children who would once have owned them explicit. And toys are not uncommon in the river. They tend to be small enough to slip away easily, they might fall in directly, or be washed from a sewer.

My friend Josh picked up a perfect seventeenth-century toy cannon when we were out together once. It would have worked faultlessly, the exquisitely formed bronze shooting out a tiny ball; it even had a hole for a fuse to light the sniff of powder. What a little banger it would have been in the hands of some well-off boy or his uncle. Holding it, I recalled the many episodes in *Tristram Shandy* in which his wounded Uncle Toby re-enacted the Siege of Namur upon his bowling green. I can also imagine the awful horror a child would have felt on losing a toy into the river. Every parent has such an incident. My son left his teddy bear (Scruffy) on the airport bus in Oslo, and cried into the night. Thank heavens for the efficiency of Scandinavian lost and found. I lost my comfort blanket under a car in Washington DC, and my parents still tell the story.

Toys are just one way in which Londoners have found comfort in hard times, or luxuriated in better, but there are many more: the luxuries only available in a metropolis, the security of hoarded cash, even the reassurance of home, however far away that is. The first piece I illustrate is just that: a Roman hypocaust tile (pages 224–5) used to provide underfloor heating to Roman villas and public buildings. Today underfloor heating is an indulgence (but *what* an indulgence); two thousand years ago it would have meant the comfort of home to Romans living on a cold wet island at the very outskirts of their empire. The Romans did not adapt the vernacular when they built London from scratch; they used Roman

'The Romans did not adapt the vernacular when they built London from scratch; they used Roman styles, Roman techniques and Roman technologies.'

styles, Roman techniques and Roman technologies. In part this can be seen as a strategy of demonstrating dominance, turning a wasteland in a tribal country into a shining metropolis, but I imagine it was just as much about providing a recognisable home for Roman expats. The same has always been used by colonists; look at Macau, or Sydney, or Granada. When people are far from their place of origin, they crave the sense-memory of home.

And London has become home to so many different cultures. The city thrives on bridging difference. Welcoming people from around the world has enormously benefited its residents. There are economic migrants (above a certain social scale, they too are expats; one day, shortly after François Hollande was elected in France, the Queen's Park playground suddenly seemed to become francophone), and there are those seeking refuge. In this, London has perhaps the greatest history. Thirty years after the doll's head came over from Thuringia, 10,000 German Jewish children arrived at Liverpool Street station through the Kindertransport. In the late-nineteenth century, Jews fleeing the Russian pogroms made their way to the East End. There, they found refuge in houses first occupied by Huguenot immigrants, French protestants fleeing persecution. Now the same houses are taken by emigrants from Bangladesh, themselves refugees from massacres in their home country. And that's just Spitalfields. What about Kilburn and the London Irish; Notting Hill and *Empire Windrush*; Chinatown. On pages 226–7 I have a perfume bottle stopper; the first London perfumers were Mediterranean immigrants to St James's.

London has also been a place of refuge and advancement for its countrymen, promising, though not always guaranteeing, safety. The Roman merchant's city was burnt to the ground by Boudica a generation after it was founded, and thereafter became increasingly militarised. From a temporary military base erected during the rebuilding, a substantial fort was built in around AD 120. Housing perhaps a thousand soldiers, the fort occupied a square almost exactly between the present Museum of London and the Guildhall. The fort's northern and western walls were coopted into the great wall around the City built from AD 200, the rest of the fort was lost. This wall held London safe on three sides, and open to the river. The city bounded by the Roman wall *was* the City of London for most of its history, barring a few illegal settlements.

Saxon invasions encouraged the rushed construction of the fourth wall along the river frontage in AD 280, but Britain was becoming less and less stable. The more uncertainty there was in the country, the more was spent by the wealthy to insulate themselves from the existential dread of it all: villas added mod cons; those by the river are known to have built rooms with hypocaust heating in this period. It is not always possible to spend your way out of trouble, and after the withdrawal of the Roman army in 410, London did not last long.

Two hundred years later, the thriving Saxon city of Lundenwic stretched south from Covent Garden to the River, well outside the boundaries of the Roman Wall. This town is remembered in the name Aldwych, the *old wic*, or the old market. The Saxon *wic* added to the Roman Londinium: each town a market town, a trading post, both relying on the tidal Thames for international import/export. Lundenwic lasted until the Vikings became too strong, and then was moved by King Alfred back within the old walls of Londinium. As mentioned in *Pleasures of the Table*, from the middle of the ninth century, Viking invaders had been attacking London as part of their great invasion of England and the ultimate establishment of the Danelaw – Danish territories that swept from Northumberland down to London. Saxons fled to the safety of London, safety that was eventually ensured, not through territorial integrity, but by buying peace from the Danish King Cnut, later King of all England.

But it wasn't just safety that brought people to London, perhaps just as important were the opportunities that it offered. Vast, internationally connected, inhabited by the richest, the poorest and everyone in between, London wrought from this scale entertainments, fashions and all the joys of consumption that were each impossible to recreate elsewhere. The same holds true today, although it is viewed with no little frustration by the rest of the country; it is an inevitable feedback loop. The more London has to offer, the more people arrive to take advantage of it, and the more they themselves bring to the capital. Today the city is desperately expensive, unaffordable to a generation of millennials, and yet still they come here from the great regional powerhouses of the country, because they believe London has the best of everything, the best jobs, the best museums, the best theatres and shops and restaurants. Internal migration, just like immigration, is self-selecting: it is people with the most entrepreneurial spirit, the most ambition, who leave the comforts (or discomforts) of home and make for the bright lights of the great Wen. The young will not stay forever, however. The Office of National Statistics shows that in their thirties, once they've made their careers and started their families, Londoners begin to move out again, to places where houses are cheaper and roads quieter.

Seven hundred years ago, the city had a population of 80,000, two orders of magnitude smaller than today. Yet it was four times larger than any other city in the country and five times as wealthy. In fourteenth-century London the King's increasing favour of Westminster as his palace of residence (Parliament travelled the country in those days, and so did the King; but in the 1300s it began to meet more regularly in Westminster) meant rich merchants and powerful nobles built their mansions nearby. Satisfying the wealthy helped bring about a concentration of craftsmen and their suppliers; brought closely together, they innovated, economised, created new and exciting luxuries, which sounds rather like present-day Silicon Valley. This is interesting, because as venture capitalist and blogger Benedict Evans points out, London was already beginning to crack a problem that Silicon Valley is still desperately trying to solve: how to get people to buy things they don't know they need. London became a city the wealthy visited especially to shop in. The rural elites came to purchase supplies for their estates, and because there was such great diversity of traders, such vital competition and collaboration, they found themselves exposed to tempting new indulgences. Today the same is true:

'Internal migration, just like immigration, is self-selecting: it is people with the most entrepreneurial spirit, the most ambition, who leave the comforts (or discomforts) of home and make for the bright lights of the great Wen.'

walk through Exmouth Market, or Lower Marsh, or Broadway Market, or the Golborne Road, or Selfridges, or even, disdainfully, Harrods. It is impossible not to be touched by a desire for something you previously never even knew existed.

Just as important as shopping to London's attraction were the entertainments the city offered, from fourteenth-century animal baiting and mummers and mystery plays to Tudor theatres, publishers and pleasure grounds. The sixteenth century marked an important cultural change for Londoners, as works of literature and theatrical performances became more accessible to members of lower social classes. In part, this came about through the determination of William Caxton, the first English printer (based in Westminster) to print works in English as well as Latin in the fifteenth century. The more common written English became, the greater were moves to standardise its spelling and grammar and the more classical (and foreign-language) works were translated. Although Caxton's primary customers were the nobility, within a few generations printed books had wormed their way into the middle classes, and original works were regularly written in English.

Reading is a small-scale comfort, solitary unless aloud. When sixteenth-century Londoners wanted to share their feelings with the crowd, they went to the theatre. Theatres were barely tolerated by a nervous state, because a crowd with its emotions roused is a dangerous

'When sixteenth-century Londoners wanted to share their feelings with the crowd, they went to the theatre. Theatres were barely tolerated by a nervous state, because a crowd with its emotions roused is a dangerous thing.'

thing. The Lord Chamberlain was censoring plays in London until 1968; in 1574 a law was passed forbidding theatres being built at all in the City of London. This is why outdoor playhouses (like the reconstructed Globe) gathered in Southwark and Shoreditch, far beyond the boundaries. These truly were the people's playhouses, open to all, and all enjoyed the vernacular plays of Shakespeare. Payment was put into little green earthenware jars that had to be smashed to count the takings (pages 228–9). There is an indirect link from the Globe through to the great Victorian musical halls: these entertainments were great levellers, open to the gallant rich and the galleries of poor, both laughing the same laughs, crying the same tears, though drinking different drinks.

Because London is home to so many people, and because London is new to so many of the people it is home to (over a third of Londoners were born outside of the UK, many more were born elsewhere in the country) and because London dominated international trade for so long, it has been able to provide its residents with the most extraordinary goods, foods and cultural pursuits. Newcomers bring a piece of home with them; craftspeople, artists and entrepreneurs discover surprising ideas and indulgent luxuries in the studio or office or workshop next door. Together, they make something new. London got bigger because it was already big, and the greater it became, the more it had to offer.

HYPOCAUST TILE

Roman, likely AD 100–300

Hinting at the luxurious life of Roman London, this tile is instantly recognisable because of its bright red clay and indented stripes. A lined red tile is almost always a hypocaust tile, used in the Roman equivalent of underfloor heating.

Roman houses were typically built over a basement, the floor supported on a grid of pillars. A furnace under the floor sent hot air circulating between the pillars – the hypocaust – while flues carried heat into the walls. Hypocausts meant rooms were toasty and evenly heated. Floors and pillars would have been made of red earthenware tiles (*terracotta*, from the Italian 'baked earth') like these.

Often hypocausts are all that remain of Roman buildings. Above the ground, many houses were made of wood, others had their stone repurposed for later building projects. The grid of pillars sunk into the ground is all that's left. Sadly lost are the mosaics that would have decorated the upper surfaces of a hypocaust floor.

Seneca was rather down on hypocausts. The Stoic thought they weakened the great Roman spirit: 'The brush of a cool breeze,' he writes, 'is dangerous for a man protected from the winter winds by proper windows, whose feet are kept comfortable with warmed blankets, regularly replaced, and given dinner in rooms with heating in the walls and the floor.'

'Well yes, but have *you* tried living in London?' the emigrant might have said. The hypocaust was an important comfort, a necessary memory of home. It's interesting, because Seneca was aware of how *other* London was. In an ode to the Emperor Claudius, he wrote, 'Britons beyond the known seas... He forced to wear Romulus's yoke'. That's us, beyond the known seas.

Today the Thames foreshore is littered with red tiles. Not all of them reveal the tell-tale stripes of the hypocaust, but many do, a testament to the many thousands that must have been produced in a defence against the British weather. The technology was forgotten when the Romans abandoned England; we reverted to clustering helplessly around fireplaces: broiled on one side, frozen on the other.

The facets of this perfume bottle stopper give it an internal light like some druidical crystal, which is probably why my son confiscated it on sight for his collection. It's missing a shank and perhaps a dauber: a long and delicate stem of glass with a tiny teardrop at the base that dipped into the perfume. Lifted out, you dabbed it on the five points: one on each wrist, either side of the jaw, and one above the cleavage if you were feeling racy.

London has been home to some of the great perfume houses, and retains that heritage. The earliest was Floris, which still fragrances the air of St James's from their original shop at 89 Jermyn Street. Like many of the early English perfumers, Floris was founded by a barber. Juan Famenias Floris came to London from Menorca and opened his barbershop in London's clubland in 1730; *en route* to London he studied perfumery in Montpellier, then the equal of Grasse. He became famous for perfumes inspired by memories of his Mediterranean homeland; Edward Bodenham, Juan's great (x7) grandson, spoke to me of fragrances as old friends, that the sense of smell has the power to transport you right back to where you first encountered it.

Floris' list of specialities prepared for the 1851 Great Exhibition included 112 perfumes 'for the handkerchief', such as 'Canterbury Wood Violets' and 'Bouquet d'Napoleon III' as well as 'inexhaustible' smelling salts and ten different types of tooth powders. The shop, and the perfumes, remain in the family; hairdressing slipped away centuries ago.

Instead, past generations had their hair cut at the barbershop directly behind Floris, Briggs in Ormond Yard. There was a Briggs perfume once, though there hasn't been a Mr Briggs since the 1950s. The shop was taken over then by Philip, now ninety-two years old, my own barber too and just as much a friend. He never lets me choose the style. I sit and he gives me 'the school-boy look'. He worked under Briggs (Mr and then Mrs) for almost a decade before taking on the shop. Also an immigrant, Philip left Cyprus in 1947, his home now Turkish territory.

Upstairs and along the road a little, a ledger in Floris' back room lies open at the orders of HRM The Duke of York, Piccadilly. Some years after the page was begun, the name was crossed out in red and replaced with HM The King, Buckingham Palace.

PERFUME BOTTLE STOPPER

Undated

TUDOR MONEY BOX

Sixteenth century

This little nipple of Tudor greenware (or nubbin, either way there's something extremely anatomical about it) is absolutely diagnostic for its original object. There is a lot of green glazed pottery on the foreshore, most of it hard to place, but finding a green finial like this means that you've found a bit of a money box. The wonderful thing about Tudor money boxes is that they were meant to be broken. They had a slit for putting money in, but no hole to get it out again. Their fragmentary end was designed into them, unlike so many of the sherds that you find as you walk stiff necked, head bent in supplication to the great treasure gods, along the gravelly beaches of the Thames.

They were about the size of a large orange: round-bellied, pear-shaped pots, looking like fat alderman. A slit bulging down the middle like a row of buttons, the knob on their necks like a hat. Maybe the knob was so you could strap the box to your waist, though it seems uncomfortable to me.

The boxes are associated with children, primarily. As Christmas apprentices sought tips in the boxes, wealthier children were given money as gifts. And when it was full, then came the SMASH (What anticipation there must have been. What joy.) and the money rolled out and the children went running off to buy sweetmeats and toys. Happy Christmas everybody.

More devious children would fish delicately around inside with a slender knife, drawing coins out one by one. And we know some of them took this cowardly route because there are money boxes that are unbroken except for cracks around their slot: sure signs that some cheeky fishing around had gone on. But mainly, money boxes are found in pieces, and it is gratifying to find them.

They weren't only for children though. Adults hid or buried them, full of coins, because there were no savings banks – and so they have become an important source of our knowledge of the coinage of the period. And, just possibly, these little pots gave us the phrase 'box office'. They were used in all theatres to collect money at the door. A penny for the ground, more for the galleries. What's your taking tonight? Manager's office, smash the boxes and get counting.

No visit to London would be complete with a trip to the V&A in South Kensington. For a mudlarker doubly so: the collections of applied arts should be the first stopping-off point in understanding where fragments fit into the whole. Its pottery galleries are a spotter's guide, an *I-Spy* for foreshore treasures: 60 points for a Bartmann jug; 30 points for delftware; David Bellamy's reassuring rhoticism playing in the background. But to see a complete version of this object, you need to go east to Bethnal Green, to the V&A Museum of Childhood.

The uncanny valley of porcelain dolls has long been exploited by the horror industry. Little is so frightening as the almost-human with agency, the fixed and friendly smile and the carving knife, the turning head, the shifting eyes. Somehow, being broken increases that fear factor. I keep this one in a shoebox. This view is from the back: you see the shoulder blade, left cheek and missing cranium. It is brainless, menacing. I could imagine it turning on me.

And yet, these dolls weren't made to scare. They were companions to children of the wealthy. The chilling stare, often glass eyes set in porcelain, was a nineteenth-century evolution of earlier wood and wax and *papier mâché*. Poorer children in the nineteenth century made do with wax heads on stuffed rag bodies or unjointed bits of bisque like the Frozen Charlotte (pages 232–3).

Two types of porcelain doll were made. China was first: painted after it was fired. Then came bisque, like this doll, where the skin tone was applied after the first firing, then fired again for a more realistic colour. Most of the doll industry was European, and Armand Marseille, based in Thuringia in Germany, was one of the largest manufacturers of bisque. At its peak, his factory was producing over a thousand dolls a day.

Mould 370 was one of their most common moulds; dolls based on the 370 were made for over thirty years. The head and shoulders remained the same while the jointed kid-leather bodies varied. They had aspirational names like Miss Millionaire and Duchess; names conjuring exquisite childhood loneliness like My Companion, My Playmate and My Dearie; and my favourite: Rosebud. Was the loss of this Rosebud into the waters of the Thames the foundation of a young girl's future just as the sleigh was to Charles Foster Kane?

BISQUE DOLL

Mould 370
Armand Marseille
1894–1920s

FROZEN CHARLOTTE

Mid- to late-nineteenth century

This little bisque doll is one of the sort known as the Frozen Charlotte, a tiny, unjointed, helpless figure. The name comes from a popular American folk song that tells the story of a girl who won't wrap up in winter because it would hide her beautiful dress, and in vanity she finds her end. I've included an excerpt of the song below. Initially Frozen Charlottes all looked alike, a little female doll, but like Google, Hoover and Heroin, the name became generic and spread to any plaything like this, cold to the touch and unresponsive.

'Why, Charlotte, dear,' her mother says,
'This blanket around you fold;
It is a dreadful night, you know,
You'll take your death of cold.'
'Oh, no! Oh, no!' young Charlotte says,
She laughed like a gypsy queen,
'To ride in blankets muffled up,
I never would be seen.' . . .

They jumped into the sleigh,
And away they rode o'er the mountain side,
And the hills so far away. . . .

And the ballroom hove in sight . . .

Driving up, young Charles jumps out,
And he offers his hand to her;
'Why sit you there like a monument
That hath no power to stir?' . . .

They tried all means 'twas in their power,
Her life for to restore,
For Charlotte's was a frozen corpse,
Ne'er to speak nevermore.

Excerpts from 'Young Charlotte'

I'd found this little Westerwald heart motif on the South Bank before going into the Tate Modern. There was a picture at the Sonia Delaunay exhibition that resonated, a dreamy portrait of another artist, seemingly surrounded by love hearts that were probably just wallpaper in the background. It seemed kitsch and Victorian – like those early Valentine's cards that simply explode filigrees and sacred hearts. The Westerwald piece – probably a jug – would have been the same: well decorated.

But Westerwald is much much earlier; the heart here is courtly and mediæval, it's an honourable symbol. So however well covered in hearts, I don't think kitsch is the right way to look at it, either for the pottery, or for Delaunay.

It is the way the glazes pool around the heart that explains, in part, why this Westerwald pottery is so often found in the River Thames. Like the Bartmann jugs on pages 86–7, this is German stoneware, probably from the seventeenth century. Both styles were extremely popular in England because they could be finely decorated and were extremely tough, and the reason for this was simple: the clay. The only clay suitable for making stoneware at the time was found in a band from the east of Belgium to the west of Poland. The best clays were in the Rhineland and the Westerwald.

Potteries clustered around the quarries and mines; proximity led to innovations and cross-fertilisations of technologies. This piece marries four great developments. The first, clay. Second was salt-glazing, which reacted with the stoneware to form a beautiful dove-grey glaze. Here salt was thrown into the kiln during firing where it instantly vaporised. It was introduced before the sixteenth century. Then in the mid-sixteenth century applied reliefs were developed in Raeren, present-day Belgium. This meant that plain pottery could suddenly be covered in accurately realised and rather complex decoration. The moulds for these came to the Westerwald alongside the Raeren potters, who set out in search of stability and profit. Lastly came colour: first cobalt blue, introduced by Jan Emens Mennicken, and then manganese purple. They complemented the dove grey perfectly.

The results were in demand throughout Europe, and exported by the hundredweight to the American colonies. Westerwald pottery was a high-tech luxury export.

WESTERWALD HEART

Salt-glazed stoneware
Late-seventeenth century

WALDORF HOTEL TEACUP

Decorated with pendant husk swags
Twentieth century

What connects this piece of tableware with our country's most treasured Nazi appeasers and the Profumo affair? A family. The Astors: one of the richest families ever to live on either side of the Atlantic.

The Waldorf Hotel was developed by a theatrical impresario, Edward Sanders. He bookended it with two theatres, the Waldorf – now the Novello – and the Aldwych. William Waldorf Astor provided the money and got the name. Twice.

The hotel is a huge Beaux-Arts building, an incredible piece of French fancy built in the new town of Aldwych – an area that had been flattened at the turn of the twentieth century and reconstructed along Haussmann's lines. It seems likely to be the home of this cup; there are other Waldorf hotels – most famously the Waldorf Astoria in New York, but I think it would be stretching credibility to attribute it to that one.

The Astor fortune originated in the fur trading of John Jacob Astor, the great-grandfather of William Waldorf. To the Astor family, making money was the quintessence of life; each generation doubled the fortune of the previous and William Waldorf was the richest man in America. In 1890, after the death of both his father and his career in politics, he moved permanently to England.

William Waldorf arrived like a conquering hero. He had a reputed $100 million to spend, and he went to town. Besides the hotel and the theatres, he bought and renovated Two Temple Place overlooking the Thames (now open to the public: go if you can); Hever Castle in Kent, where Anne Boleyn had lived; and Cliveden, from the Duke of Westminster. He bought himself up a media empire (including the *Observer*) and a peerage. He was ennobled, first Baron, and then Viscount Astor.

And he wasn't the best of them. His son, plain Waldorf Astor, inherited much of the empire and Cliveden House, where he set up home with his wife Nancy Astor. Nancy was the first woman to sit as an MP, a staunch anti-semite, and the hostess of the Cliveden Set – a group of aristocrats who met at the house to formulate an English style of Fascism. In 1961, their son Bill (William Waldorf Astor II) hosted a party at Cliveden. Around the pool, the Secretary of State for War, John Profumo, spotted a topless Christine Keeler. We've all seen that Lewis Morley photo of her with the Arne Jacobsen chair. How could he resist? Two years later, the affair blew up and took the government with it.

SO YOU WANT TO
GO MUDLARKING?

THE JOYS
OF
MUDLARKING

If you've read this far, and you live in London, or you've ever been to London, or you think that you might go one day to London, and you're not tempted to just take a look at the Thames one day and see if the tide is out, then you must have a heart of Antarctic stone. There is no activity that I can think of where the rank amateur, or a family out in town for the day, can step instantaneously into another world and return home holding something that's been lost for centuries. Metal detecting needs specialist equipment, training, the willingness to walk unforgiving fields in the rain. I've seen Detectorists, *I know what it's like. Mudlarking, in my mind, is like detecting for pleasure. It's an activity for everyone, rewarding for everyone. I hope that you'll give it a go.*

The first thing to be said about mudlarking is that anyone, absolutely anyone, can go down to the foreshore and find a piece of history.

The second thing to say is that there are responsibilities. The objects lying on the beaches are fragments of London's history, and some of them are important. In a way that I hope doesn't sound jingoistic, they are our heritage – everybody's heritage – and there is I think a moral obligation to ensure that what you find on the beach adds to our understanding and relationship with the past. There's also a legal obligation: anything of interest needs to be recorded by archaeologists. You can't dig on the foreshore without a permit.

I don't want to frighten anyone off, so I'll just put that there for now and come back to details in a little while. The important thing to remember is, whatever anyone says, you are free to go down to almost any part of the foreshore without any sort of a licence, but there are restrictions and responsibilities.

There are two ways to go mudlarking: impulsively, and with planning. If you're anywhere near the river and you look over and see that the tide is out, look for a way down and walk a moment on the beach. You're already in a place that 90 per cent of Londoners have never been. Breath the air. Listen to the silence. It is an unrecognisable London, a ghost road cut through the most populous city in Europe. That is the first sensation. History has nothing to do with it, it is the passing through a portal into a different town. Exponentially more so than the parks, it is London's *rus in urbe*. If you're being impulsive, don't be so free of care that you ignore an incoming tide and get yourself drowned. The water can come

'The important thing to remember is, whatever anyone says, you are free to go down to almost any part of the foreshore without any sort of licence, but there are restrictions and responsibilities.'

in quickly and cut off your escape. Know how you're getting back out again. Don't drown yourself in a mudtrap either. The ground is solid most everywhere, but there are places that it isn't. Walk tentatively. Don't lose your boots.

If you want to assure yourself of a mudlarking session, you need to plan to go when the tides are out. The Port of London Authority (PLA) has a website with all the tide tables for the year. Have a look for them. The times for London Bridge will give you all you need for a first-time trip. Choose your month and be aware of British Summer Time – the tide tables give times in GMT throughout the year, so you'll need to add an hour in summer. The tables show four times per day: two high tides and two low (high will be 6 or 7 point something, low should be 0 point something to make it worthwhile. The lower the better). I tend to arrive at the water an hour before low tide, and then stay an hour after. I haven't the concentration for more than two hours staring at pebbles.

With your date and time set, you can pack. I just bring a couple of plastic bags (without holes, so I don't lose little things or soak everything with slowly dripping mud) and some gloves (latex, double layered; Marigolds if you're feeling dashing; I use semi-rubberised work gloves). I also bring a trowel, but I've got the permit. You can get away dressing like you would in town, but I prefer boots and trousers I don't care so much about. There's likely to be a bit of mud gathering about the ankles, and it's up to you entirely which trousers you'd like it to gather on. I wear hiking boots. Some people wear wellies. I've worn a suit and Oxford brogues when I couldn't bear to miss a serendipitous low tide.

Then there's the question of where? I can't recommend highly enough the beach in front of the Tate Modern for the first-time mudlarker. It has everything: it's easy to get down to; you can find as good an object there as anywhere; and when you're done, there's a fantastic gallery just above you at which to wash your hands, enjoy the art and have lunch. There's a host of other restaurants nearby, too, just on the way to Southwark. To get there take the Tube to Southwark station and follow the directions to the Tate. Almost directly in front of the gallery there's a gate incorporated into the railings that opens onto a wide staircase to the river. There are two other stairs, one slightly further west and another right by the Globe Theatre. The Globe stairs are the easiest to spot but for some reason I prefer to leave by those stairs rather than enter. It's a personal habit.

Enjoy the first crunch of your feet on gravel. I'm sure you've been to the seaside before. It's like going to the seaside. Have a look at the beach. If you look carefully you'll see that the tide sorts the gravel and pebbles of the foreshore by size – there are stripes or strata of different materials: bands of big stones and bands of small. The small fades into sand. In amongst the grey stones you might see stripes of black coal. The best place to look, at first, is along these interstices of the strata. Where one band ends and another begins is where the tide will have rolled objects and dropped them.

If you've come down the middle steps, head east underneath the Tate following one of the bands. Stop every now and again to look around you and see if anywhere else looks more profitable. If you're a gravel kicking sort of person, kick your toe into the gravel a little. You won't find anything but it will feel good.

You will see a lot of pottery. There are places where there is so much broken pottery that the ripples of the river make it ring like bells. Turn everything over. Like buttered toast, pottery always lands pattern side down. Pick up anything you think is beautiful. Look out for pipe stems – they're the only tubes you'll see and there are lots of them. Pick one up. It's probably two hundred years old and no one's touched it since some Jack Tar threw his broken pipe over the side of his ship. Pick them all up. Pipe stems are wonderful. I made a sort of Arte Povera canvas with the first fifty pipe stems I found. They were all I found, once.

As you get under the giant bankside emblazoned on the river wall, notice the shelves of mud sticking over the surface. They hold treasures and you're not allowed to dig in them. I don't think you'd want to, either. Thames mud is heavy, sticky and perfumed. But each tide washes new objects out. Look around beneath the shelves. There will be lots of rusty nails, and that's a surprisingly interesting sign. Metal gathers together on the beaches – something to do with the way the fluid mechanics of the river acts on objects of a similar density I imagine – so have a good look around the nails. If you're really lucky you'll pick out Tudor pins, or buttons, or a coin.

Take home whatever you like. I clean my finds with dilute Milton sterilising fluid and a toothbrush. A doctor who collects spittoons recommended it. I figure I'm never going to stick them in my mouth. Then, when you've laid your finds out in front of you, you can enjoy knolling everything you've found. Think about what to research further, what may be important enough to report. The best places to start your research are with the database of the PAS (Portable Antiquities Scheme) and with the V&A and the Museum of London, comparing what you've found with their incredible collections of decorative arts. It's all online.

Everything on the Thames foreshore belongs to the PLA (except where it belongs to the Crown). It does not mind the amateur mudlarks' beachcombing habits but it has restrictions in place to preserve the archaeology. The most important obligation is reporting your interesting finds. The PAS was set up to ensure historical finds were recorded for later study. It means you get to keep what you find, almost always, but if it's important enough you need to hand it over to a Finds Liaison Officer (FLO) to be recorded. Unless it's extraordinary, it will be returned afterwards. The PAS is primarily interested in objects from before 1650, so if you've got anything that you think meets that criterion, look up its website and see how to contact the London FLO. Send an email with a photograph and you'll be able to make an appointment to have it recorded at the Museum of London. I find this to be the most exquisite exercise in disappointment. Self-identified Roman pottery is demoted to post-mediæval; mediæval jewellery to Regency. For all that, it is better to over-report than under.

A few other aspects of mudlarking that you should bear in mind. I've made it sound like you can mudlark just about anywhere, and you pretty much can. However, there are areas that are restricted, whether as Scheduled Ancient Monuments or for other reasons. In particular, mudlarking in front of the Tower of London is out. So is Queenhithe and Greenwich Palace. That's why I recommend the South Bank. From Waterloo to the Tate, there is nothing but joy and delight to be had (except for the very sticky bit just east of Waterloo Bridge).

If you would like to mudlark with others, there are plenty of groups that offer tours, but perhaps the best way to get involved is through the Foreshore Recording & Observation Groups (FROGS). These groups are run by volunteers under the Thames Discovery Programme (TDP) giving you the opportunity to work with others to help ensure that the Thames foreshore is preserved and recorded. Take a look at the FROG blog first for really fascinating features about the river and its history. When I spoke to Nathalie Cohen, who is Head of Community Archaeology at MOLA (Museum of London Archaeology) and leads the TDP, she enthused about how accessible and diverse are the FROGS. They fulfil Ivor Noël Hume's wish for the Thames, that bodies 'would patrol their own shores and so preserve for the nation the treasure that still lies there'.

The restrictions are minor and not onerous. The opportunities wonderful. The river is yours as much as anybody's and mudlarking is the most fun you can have with your wellies on. Good luck and good hunting.

AFTERWORD
BRIGITTE SCHMIDT

Family photographs
Twentieth and twenty-first centuries

My last object closes the impossible circle. Every other piece has been lost and is now found: a narrative arc, but not a complete one. Artefacts cannot be returned to people dead a hundred years. These photographs are important to me because I could give them back.

On 1 August 2015, when I was driving to Dorset with my family to spend some of our summer on the Jurassic Coast, Brigitte Schmidt was enjoying her second day in London. It was her first time visiting from Germany, and on Westminster Bridge her wallet was stolen from her backpack.

Two months later, right under Tower Bridge, I picked the wallet up. It was empty of money, but full of keepsakes and included a postal address. I took them home, dried them and sent them back to Brigitte with a letter explaining my project. She emailed me four days later; opening that email was as exciting as any find. Much more emotional. 'Yesterday was my birthday and just on this day your letter was in my mailbox. . . . I opened the letter and saw the surprise . . . tears are running over my face . . . as you wrote, the sentimental value are the pictures, certainly this one from my Dad, because he died in 2007 and I have only less pictures from him.' It had, she wrote, been 'very crowded and a lot of thimble-riggers and jack-puddings were on the Bridge'. For the gift of those words alone, it was worth returning the wallet.

Brigitte told me her story. Her parents had divorced when she was three; for almost her entire life she had no contact with her father at all, and then, when he was very ill, Brigitte was asked to look after him. They 'had communication only with the eyes and with the help of our hands – but what could I say – this was a very precious time. . . . We had nearly two wonderful years together, than Dad passed away and I arranged an honourable goodbye celebration with all my friends for him. The other pictures are also of my family – Mum, my husband, my brother, my niece . . . all the people I love and are important for me.'

Artefacts make us ask what we will leave behind. Not through a fear of death or a fear of being forgotten, but perhaps as substitute for a harder question: who are we? *Are* we what we leave behind? Does the river take our stories with us, or can they ever be found? Can our stories be brought back again?

ACKNOWLEDGEMENTS

I would like to thank my parents, Bob and Judy Sandling, for supporting me throughout all my career twists and literary endeavours. Clare Sandling's encouragement and belief kept me writing; Milo Sandling's unalloyed excitement and hungry appetite for new finds ensure I keep going back to the river.

I have spent time by the Thames with some very dear friends. I would like to thank them for the conversation and ideas that we enjoy there. Josh Edmonds, who has accompanied me on so many walks besides the river; Jamie Collingridge who planted the seed for this book in my mind and Nic McElhatton who collects as eagerly as I do.

Thank you to those who offered comments and advice on parts of early drafts: Lucy Soutter, Dominic Eliot and all at WOOA. Thank you to Julia Muggenburg for that first gem of recognition that I had something worth writing about.

I've worked with many experts in identifying objects in this book. I'm eternally grateful for their insight, advice, and reading lists. Where pieces are correctly identified, it is down to them; if there are misattributions, they are my fault. Special thanks go to Jacqui Pearce and Rodney Woolley who have helped enormously with identifying my pottery finds. Thanks to Marco Almeida for identifying Chinese porcelain. Thanks to Ian Betts and James Wright of Museum of London Archaeology.

I appreciate that many of the people who work with the river and the foreshore have been willing to talk to me for this book. Thanks to Nathalie Cohen of MOLA for her generosity of time and thoughts in discussing the activities of the Thames Discovery Programme. I am grateful to Jane Sidell of Historic England for providing me with not only a fascinating history lesson but also views on the Thames as a flow of ancient monuments. The Port of London Authority own much of the foreshore and manage access, thank you to Martin Garside of the PLA for discussing how the river is licensed, and thank you to the PLA for providing such useful tide tables, even if their primary purpose is not for mudlarks' advantage.

So much data from mudlarking would be lost without the Portable Antiquities Scheme, and I am especially grateful to Michael Lewis, Head of the PAS, for a detailed background to the scheme and his views on the river. Without London's Finds Liaison Officer, Kate Sumnall, I would not have had the first idea about anything; I'd like to thank her for her encouragement and gentle let-downs of my over-enthusiastic identifications over the past years.

Thank you to all those who were generous with their knowledge as I researched this book. Edward Bodenham of Floris, Richard Edgcumbe of the V&A, Steve McManus of the English Ceramic Circle, Peter Finch of the River Thames Society, Stephen Freeth of the Vintners' Company and Henry Jeffreys for an excellent drinking reading list, Ben Malkin and Sara Plumbly. Hakuei Wakiya of the NYK Museum in Yokohama has been extremely helpful with the history of the NYK ship's pottery; Donna Lloyd of Morgan PLC the same with the history of the Morgan Crucible Company. My thanks to Amal Gunasena of SOAS for identifying the *suraya* as Sinhalese; my especial thanks to Liya and Oreen Silva for their hospitality and efforts in researching the traditions around *suraya*s.

I would like to thank the people that I met in these stories: Sara Cannizzaro and Peter Harman; Geoffrey Munn has been both generous and encouraging. I thank Fylaktis Philippou, 'Philip', for many years of friendship and haircuts. Lastly, thank you to Brigitte Schmidt for agreeing to become my afterword.

At Frances Lincoln, thanks to Glenn Howard for his imaginative and sensitive design and Michael Brunström for thoughtful editing. I would never have been able to write this book without the support, good sense and good humour of my publisher, Andrew Dunn. Lastly I want to thank Domenica More Gordon for taking these fragments and bringing them to life with her truly beautiful illustrations.

BIBLIOGRAPHY

Ackroyd, Peter *London: The Biography* (Vintage, London, 2001)

Addison, Joseph *The Works of the Right Honourable Joseph Addison*, Volume 2, T. Cadell and W. Davies (eds) (London, 1811)

Adler, Beatrix *Early Stoneware Steins from the Les Paul Collection* (Krüger Druck + Verlag, Dillingen, 2005)

Atkins, Peter (ed.) *Beastly Urban Histories* (Ashgate, Aldershot, 2012)

Ayto, Eric G. *Clay Tobacco Pipes* (Shire Publications, Princes Risborough, 2002)

Bacon, Francis *The Works of Francis Bacon: Lord Chancellor of England* Basil Montagu (ed.) (William Pickering, London, 1826)

Barker, David & Crompton, Steve *Slipware in the Collection of The Potteries Museum & Art Gallery* (A & C Black, London, 2007)

Barnard, Julian *Victorian Ceramic Tiles* (Christie's South Kensington Collectors Series, London, 1979)

Barnett, David *London: Hub of the Industrial Revolution* (I.B. Taurus, London, 1998)

Bell, Sandra 'The Subject of Smoke: Tobacco in Early Modern England' in *The Mysterious and the Foreign* Helen Ostovich, Mary V. Silcox, and Graham Roebuck (eds) (University of Delaware Press, Newark, DE, 2008)

Betts, Ian M. & Weinstein, Rosemary I. *Tin-Glazed Tiles from London* (Museum of London Archaeology, London, 2010)

Billings, E.R. *Tobacco, Its History, Varieties, Culture, Manufacture and Commerce* (American Publishing Company, Hartford, CN, 1875)

Bird, Joanna, Hassall, Mark & Sheldon, Harvey (eds) *Interpreting Roman London: Papers in memory of Hugh Chapman* (Oxbow Books, Oxford, 1996)

Blacker, J.F. *The A.B.C. of English Salt-Glaze Stone-Ware: From Dwight to Doulton* (Stanley Paul, London, 1922)

Blackmore, Lyn, Hårdh, Birgitta & Larsson, Lars (eds) 'The Origins and Growth of Lundenwic, a Mart of Many Nations: Central Places in the Migration and Merovingian Periods' in *Papers from the 52nd Sachsensymposium* (Lund, 2001)

Blocker, Jack S., Fahey, David M. & Tyrrell, Ian R. (eds) *Alcohol and Temperance in Modern History: A Global Encyclopedia* (ABC-CLIO, Santa Barbara, CA, 2003)

Bloom, Clive *Violent London: 2000 years of Riots, Rebels and Revolts* (Palgrave Macmillan, Basingstoke, 2010)

Bond, Barbara *Great Escapes: The Story of MI9's Second World War Escape and Evasion Maps* (Collins, Glasgow, 2015)

Bonfiglioli, Kyril *All the Tea in China* (Black Spring Press, London, 1996)

Britton, Frank *London Delftware* (Jonathan Horne, London, 1987)

Burke, Edmund *The Annual Register* (London, 1764)

Burnet, Gilbert *History of His Own Time* (London, 1724)

Burnett, John *Liquid Pleasures: A Social History of Drinks in Modern Britain* (Routledge, London, 1999)

Burton, William *A History and Description of English Earthenware and Stoneware* (Cassell, London, 1904)

Caple, Christopher 'The Detection and Definition of an Industry: The English Medieval and Post Medieval Pin Industry' in *Archaeological Journal* 148 (1991)

Chamberlaine, William *The Life of Mr Thomas Cooke* (London, 1814)

Cherry, Bridget & Pevsner, Nikolaus *The Buildings of England: London 3: North West* (Yale University Press, New Haven, CT, 2002)

Conte-Helm, Marie *Japan and the North East of England: From 1862 to the Present Day* (Bloomsbury, London, 1989)

Croad, Stephen *Liquid History: The Thames Through Time* (Batsford, London, 2003)

Culpeper, Nicholas *Pharmacopoeia Londinensis, or the London Dispensatory* (London, 1653)

Cunnington, Cecil Willett & Phillis *Handbook of English Costume in the Eighteenth Century* (Faber & Faber, London, 1964)

Dennet, Daniel C. *Darwin's Dangerous Idea: Evolution and the Meanings of Life* (Penguin, London, 1995)

Dickens, Charles 'A Plated Article' in *Household Words* (London, 1852)

Digby, Kenelm *The Closet of Sir Kenelm Digby Knight Opened* (London, 1669)

Doré, Gustave & Jerrold, Blanchard *London* (David & Charles Reprints, Newton Abbot, Devon, 1971)

Dumbrell, Roger *Understanding Antique Wine Bottles* (Antique Collectors' Club, Woodbridge, 1983)

Earnshaw, Steven *The Pub in Literature* (Manchester University Press, Manchester, 2000)

Ellis, Markman, Coulton, Richard & Mauger, Matthew *Empire of Tea: The Asian Leaf that Conquered the World* (Reaktion Books, London, 2015)

Findlen, Paula (ed.) *Early Modern Things: Objects and their Histories, 1500–1800* (Routledge, Abingdon, 2013)

Fortey, Richard A. *The Hidden Landscape: A Journey into the Geological Past* (The Bodley Head, London, 2010)

Foxe, John *Book of Martyrs* (1563)

Garner, F.H. & Archer, Michael *English Delftware* (Faber & Faber, London, 1972)

Glanville, Philippa *Silver in England* (Routledge, Abingdon, 2006)

Godden, Geoffrey A. *British Pottery* (Barrie & Jenkins, London, 1990)

Gulik, Robert van *The Willow Pattern*, (Heinemann, London, 1969)

Hahn, Hans Peter, Cless, Karlheinz & Soentgen, Jens (eds) *People at the Well: Kinds, Usages and Meanings of Water in a Global Perspective* (Campus Verlag, Frankfurt, 2012)

Hardwick, Paul *English Medieval Misericords: The Margins of Meaning* (The Boydell Press, Woodbridge, 2011)

Harrison, William *The Description of England* (London, 1587)

Hilton, Matthew *Smoking in British Popular Culture 1800–2000: Perfect Pleasures* (Manchester University Press, Manchester, 2000)

Hourihane, Colum (ed.) *The Grove Encyclopedia of Medieval Art and Architecture*, Volume 2 (Oxford University Press, Oxford, 2012)

Hudson, Briony *English Delftware Drug Jars: The Collection of the Museum of the Pharmaceutical Society of Great Britain* (Pharmaceutical Press, London, 2006)

Hume, Ivor Noël *Early English Delftware from London and Virginia* (The Colonial Williamsburg Foundation, Virginia, 1977)

_____ *If These Pots Could Talk: Collecting 2,000 Years of British Household Pottery* (Chipstone, New England, 2001)

_____ *Treasure in the Thames* (Frederick Muller, London, 1956)

Hurst, John G., Neal, David S. & Van Beuningen, J.J.E. *Pottery Produced and Traded in North-West Europe 1350–1650* (Stichting 'Het Nederlandse Gebruiksvoorwerp', Rotterdam, 1986)

Hutchinson, Mark & Wolffe, John *A Short History of Global Evangelicalism* (Cambridge University Press, Cambridge, 2012)

Hutton, Clayton *Official Secret: The Remarkable Story of Escape Aids, Their Invention, Production, and the Sequel* (Max Parrish, London, 1960)

Janssens, Koen H.A. (ed.) *Modern Methods for Analysing Archaeological and Historical Glass* (Wiley, Chichester, 2013)

Jones, Olive R. 'Cylindrical English Wine
and Beer Bottles, 1735–1850' in *Studies
in Archaeology, Architecture and History*
(Ottawa, 1986)

Kirkham, Pat, Mace, Rodney & Porter, Julia
*Furnishing the World: The East London
Furniture Trade, 1830–1980* (Journeyman,
London, 1987)

Lee, Paula Young (ed.) *Meat, Modernity, and the
Rise of the Slaughterhouse* (University of
New Hampshire Press, New Hampshire,
2008)

Lemmen, Hans van *Delftware Tiles* (Shire
Library, Oxford, 2010)

_____ *5000 Years of Tiles* (British Museum
Press, London, 2013)

Linscott, Eloise Hubbard (ed.) *Folk Songs of Old
New England* (Macmillan, New York, 1939)

Macdonald, Helen *H is for Hawk* (Jonathan
Cape, London, 2014)

Markham, Gervase *The English Housewife*
(London, 1615)

Mayhew, Henry *London Labour & the London
Poor* (Oxford University Press, Oxford, 2010)

McNamara, Kenneth J. *The Star-Crossed
Stone: The Secret Life, Myths, and History
of a Fascinating Fossil* (University of Chicago
Press, Chicago, 2011)

Melton, James Van Horn *The Rise of the
Public in Enlightenment Europe* (Cambridge
University Press, Cambridge, 2001)

Misson, Henri M. *Misson's Memoirs and
Observations in his Travels over England,
with Some Account of Scotland and Ireland,
Written Originally in French and Translated
by Mr Ozell* (London, 1719)

Morgan, Roy *Sealed Bottles: Their History and
Evolution (1630–1930)* (Midlands Antique
Bottle Publishing, Burton-on-Trent, 1977)

Munn, Geoffrey C. *Tiaras: A History of
Splendour* (Antique Collectors' Club,
Woodbridge 2001)

O'Connell, John *The Book of Spice: From Anise
to Zedoary* (Profile Books, London, 2015)

'Oyster Day' in *The London Saturday Journal*, 6
August 1842

Parker, Matthew *The Sugar Barons*
(Hutchinson, London, 2011)

Partridge, Eric & Beale, Paul (eds) *Dictionary
of Slang and Unconventional English*
(Routledge, Abingdon, 2000)

Pennell, Sara 'Great Quantities of
Gooseberry Pie and Baked Clod of Beef:
Victualling and Eating Out in Early Modern
London' in Paul Griffiths and Mark Jenner
(eds) *Londinopolis*, (Manchester University
Press, Manchester, 2000)

Penzer, Norman M. 'Scroll Salts' in *Apollo
Annual* (1949)

Pepys, Samuel *The Diary of Samuel Pepys*
R.C. Latham and W. Matthews (eds)
(HarperCollins, London, 2010)

Perring, Dominic *Roman London* (Routledge,
Abingdon, 1991)

Pinker, Steven *The Blank Slate* (Penguin,
London, 2003)

_____ *The Better Angels of Our Nature*
(Penguin, London, 2012)

Pugh, Peter *A Global Presence: The Morgan
Crucible Story* (Icon Books, London, 2006)

Rackham, Bernard *Medieval English Pottery*
(Faber & Faber, London, 1972)

Reeves, Peter (ed.) *The Encyclopedia of
the Sri Lankan Diaspora* (Didier Millet,
Singapore, 2014)

Rhead, G. Woolliscroft & Frederick Alfred,
Staffordshire Pots and Potters (EP
Publishing, Wakefield, 1977)

Ross, Cathy & Clark, John *London: The
Illustrated History* (Penguin, London, 2011)

Rowsome, Peter *Londinium: A New Map
and Guide to Roman London* (Museum of
London Archaeology, London, 2011)

Schwarz, L.D. *London in the Age of
Industrialisation* (Cambridge University
Press, Cambridge, 1992)

Scodel, Joshua *Excess and the Mean in
Early Modern English Literature* (Princeton
University Press, Princeton, 2002)

Seneca, *Seneca: Selected Dialogues and
Consolations* Peter J. Anderson (trans.)
(Hackett Publishing Company, Indianapolis,
IN, 2015)

Seneca, *Anger, Mercy, Revenge* Robert A.
Kaster and Martha C. Nussbaum (trans.)
(University of Chicago Press, Chicago, 2010)

Sim, Alison *Food and Feast in Tudor England*, (The History Press, Stroud, 2011)

Simon, André L. *Bottlescrew Days: Wine Drinking in England during the Eighteenth Century* (Duckworth, London, 1926)

Sinclair, Iain *Lights Out for the Territory* (Penguin, London, 2003)

Smith, Adam *An Inquiry into the Nature and Causes of the Wealth of Nations*, Volume 1 (London, 1801)

Smyth, Adam (ed.) *A Pleasing Sinne: Drink and Conviviality in Seventeenth-century England* (D.S. Brewer, Cambridge, 2004)

Stott, Rebecca *Oyster* (Reaktion Books, London, 2004)

Surtees, Robert Smith *Jorrocks' Jaunts and Jollities* (J. M. Dent & Sons, London, 1928)

_____ *Handley Cross* (George G. Harrap, London, 1930)

Tacitus, *The Annals of Tacitus*, Book XIV (Loeb Classical Library, Cambridge, MS, 1937)

Thomas, Chris (ed.) *London's Archaeological Secrets: A World City Revealed* (Yale University Press in association with the Museum of London Archaeology Service, London, 2003)

Thornbury, Walter *Old and New London: Volume 3* (Cassell, Petter & Galpin, London, 1878)

The Tract Primer, American Tract Society, (New York, NY, c.1850)

Travitsky, Betty & Prescott, Anne Lake *Seventeenth-Century English Recipe Books: Cooking, Physic and Chirurgery in the Works of W.M. and Queen Henrietta Maria, and of Mary Tillinghast*, ed. Elizabeth Spiller (Ashgate, Aldershot, 2008)

Tyler, Kieron, Betts, Ian & Stephenson, Roy *London's Delftware Industry: The Tin-Glazed Pottery Industries of Southwark and Lambeth* (Museum of London Archaeology, London, 2008)

Walvin, James *Fruits of Empire: Exotic Produce and British Taste, 1660–1800* (Macmillan, London, 1997)

Ward, John *Romano-British Buildings and Earthworks* (Methuen, London, 1911)

Whitwood, Will *Art and Mystery of Vintners and Wine-Coopers* (London, 1682)

Withington, Phil 'Intoxicants and Society in Early Modern England' in *The Historical Journal* 54 (2011)

Woodcock, Thomas & Enright, Dominique *Legal Habits: A Brief Sartorial History of Wig, Robe, and Gown* (Good Books, London, 2003)

Wray, William D. *Mitsubishi and the N.Y.K., 1870–1914: Business Strategy in the Japanese Shipping Industry* (The Council on East Asian Studies at Harvard University, Cambridge, MA, 1984)

Wright, James 'Victoria Tower Gardens: Thames Foreshore Architectural Fragments, Westminster, SW1P' in *Museum of London Archaeology* (London, 2014), unpublished report

INDEX

Entries in *italics* refer to photographs.